Forty Years of Medical Racism

Forty Years of Medical Racism:
The Tuskegee Experiments

Lucent Library of Black History

Michael V. Uschan

LUCENT BOOKS

An imprint of Thomson Gale, a part of The Thomson Corporation

THOMSON
GALE

Detroit • New York • San Francisco • San Diego • New Haven, Conn.
Waterville, Maine • London • Munich

THOMSON

GALE

To Dr. Daniel Donovan, a physician who treats the people he cares for as human beings and not simply patients.

On cover: An unidentified man is X-rayed by technicians during the Tuskegee study, a decades-long investigation of the effects of syphilis on African American males.

LIBRARY OF CONGRESS CATALOGING-IN-PUBLICATION DATA

Uschan, Michael V., 1948–
  Forty Years of Medical Racism / by Michael V. Uschan.
    p. cm. — (Lucent Library of Black History)
  Includes bibliographical references and index.
  ISBN 1-59018-486-6 (hardcover : alk. paper)
  1. Human experimentation in medicine—Alabama—Macon County—History—Juvenile literature. 2. Tuskegee Syphilis Study—Juvenile literature. 3. Syphilis—Research—Alabama—Macon County—History—Juvenile literature. 4. Syphilis—Alabama—Macon County—History—Juvenile literature. 5. African American men—Diseases—Alabama—Macon County—History—Juvenile literature. I. Tuskegee Institute. II. Title. III. Series.
R853.H8U82 2004
174.2'8'0976149—dc22
                                                          2004010678

Printed in the United States of America

Contents

Foreword

It has been more than five hundred years since Africans were first brought to the New World in shackles, and over 140 years since slavery was formally abolished in the United States. Over 50 years have passed since the fallacy of "separate but equal" was obliterated in the American courts, and some forty years since the watershed Civil Rights Act of 1965 guaranteed the rights and liberties of all Americans, especially those of color. Over time, these changes have become celebrated landmarks in American history. In the twenty-first century, African American men and women are politicians, judges, diplomats, professors, deans, doctors, artists, athletes, business owners, and home owners. For many, the scars of the past have melted away in the opportunities that have been found in contemporary society. Observers such as Peter N. Kirsanow, who sits on the U.S. Commission of Civil Rights, point to these accomplishments and conclude, "The growing black middle class may be viewed as proof that most of the civil rights battles have been won."

In spite of these legal victories, however, prejudice and inequality have persisted in American society. In 2003, African Americans comprised just 12 percent of the nation's population, yet accounted for 44 percent of its prison inmates and 24 percent of its poor. Racially motivated hate crimes continue to appear on the pages of major newspapers in many American cities. Furthermore, many African Americans still experience either overt or muted racism in their daily lives. A 1996 study undertaken by Professor Nancy Krieger of the Harvard School of Public Health, for example, found that 80 percent of the African American participants reported having experienced racial discrimination in one or more settings, including at work or school, applying for housing and medical care, from the police or in the courts, and on the street or in a public setting.

It is for these reasons that many believe the struggle for racial equality and justice is far from over. These episodes of discrimination threaten to shatter the illusion that America has completely overcome its racist past, causing many black Americans to become increasingly frustrated and confused. Scholar and writer Ellis Cose has described this splintered state in the following way: "I have done everything I was supposed to do. I have stayed out of trouble with the law, gone to the right schools, and worked myself nearly to death. What more do they want? Why in God's name won't they accept me as a full human being?" For Cose and others, the struggle for equality and justice has yet to be fully achieved.

In many subtle yet important ways the traumatic experiences of slavery and segregation continue to inform the way race is discussed and experienced in the twenty-first century. Indeed, it is possible that America will always grapple with the fallout from its distressing past. Ulric Haynes, dean of the Hofstra University School of Business has said, "Perhaps race will always matter, given the historical circumstances under which we came to this country." But studying this past and understanding how it contributes to present-day dialogues about race and history in America is a critical component of contemporary education. To this end, the Lucent Library of Black History offers a thorough look at the experiences that have shaped the black community and the American people as a whole. Annotated bibliographies provide readers with ideas for further research, while fully documented primary and secondary source quotations enhance the text. Each book in the series explores a different episode of black history; together they provide students with a wealth of information as well as launching points for further study and discussion.

A Case of Medical Racism

On July 25, 1972, people across the United States were horrified to learn that for forty years the federal government had been conducting a medical study using some of the nation's most vulnerable citizens as subjects. As the details emerged, it became clear that government doctors had ignored medical ethics concerning research involving humans. Moreover, the fact that all six hundred participants were poor, uneducated African Americans meant that the government that was supposed to protect all its citizens had in fact been taking advantage of those most in need of its care. The doctors who ran the study were trying to learn more about syphilis, a deadly sexually transmitted disease. They allowed the disease to eventually kill many of the four hundred infected men. In addition to denying the sick men treatment that could have eased the terrible symptoms of syphilis and possibly saved their lives, government doctors also kept from them the fact that they were subjects in a medical study. Moreover, the doctors made a point of not telling the men the exact nature of their illness.

A Deadly Disease

The researchers knew from the beginning that failing to treat the infected men would have deadly consequences. Syphilis was one of the most devastating diseases known to humankind, one that could lead to heart failure, loss of muscular control, blindness, insanity, and, ultimately, death. Syphilis was also one of the most feared diseases because there was no effective cure for it until the late 1940s, when penicillin became available to the general public. A comment in 1916 by Captain Edward B. Vedder of the U.S. Army Medical Corps indicates the magnitude of the danger syphilis once posed: "Syphilis is a greater menace to the public health than any other single infectious disease, not even excepting tuberculosis."[1]

Because syphilis was such a menace, the U.S. Public Health Service (PHS) was anxious to study ways of controlling the disease. In fact, what became known as the Tuskegee study was the successor to another study whose intent was to learn how to reduce the frequency of syphilis outbreaks in a population—blacks in the rural South—who appeared particularly vulnerable to infection with the disease. But at some point the purpose

A doctor draws blood from a Tuskegee study subject. Over the course of four decades, hundreds of poor, uneducated African Americans unwittingly participated in a study of the long-term effects of syphilis.

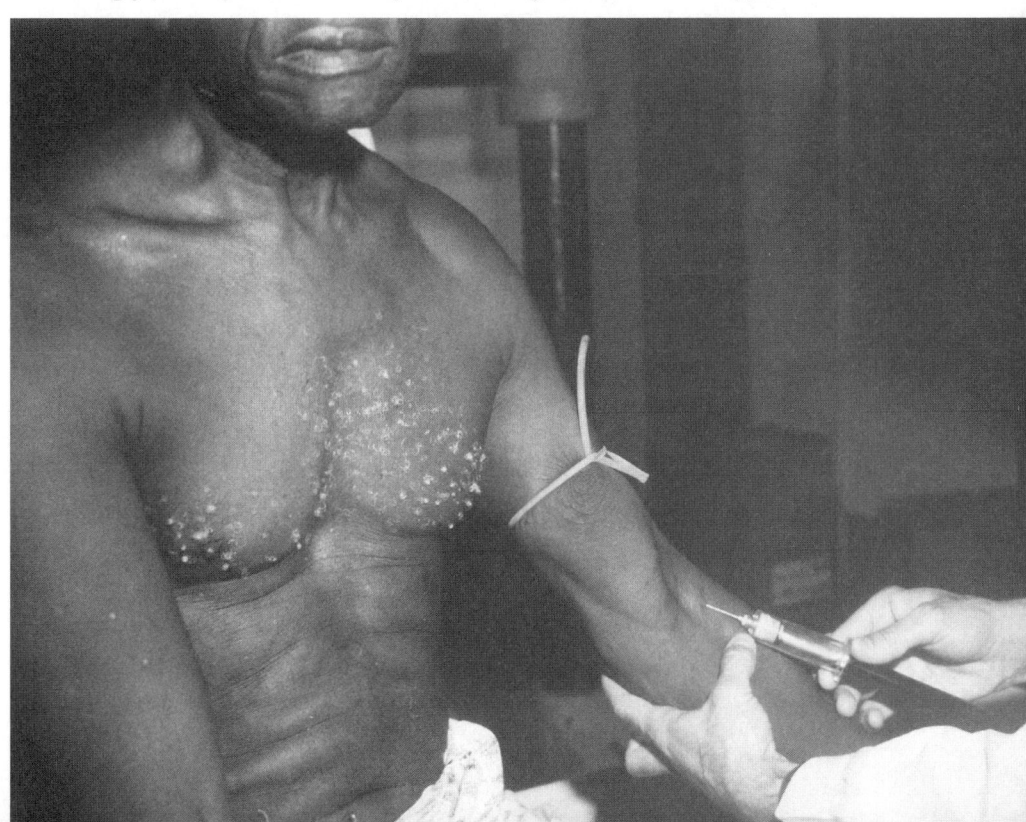

changed from controlling a dreaded disease to documenting the effects of the illness. What made the government researchers' actions even more indefensible was that all of the men in the study were black. Herman Shaw, who was involved in the study for its entire forty-year span, said, "You know this was racist. They only used colored people."[2]

"They Never Mentioned Syphilis to Me"

The research project that Shaw participated in was officially known as the Tuskegee Study of Untreated Syphilis in the Negro Male. It was named after the Tuskegee Institute in Tuskegee, Alabama, where most of the physical examinations of the men were conducted. Lasting for four decades, the Tuskegee study was the longest nontherapeutic study of human disease in medical history. In a nontherapeutic study, test subjects are observed but not treated for an illness to enable researchers to study how the disease affects people. In fact, the study was planned to run until all the subjects died. Autopsies of their bodies, which could provide detailed evidence of the physical damage the disease had done to the men, were a vital part of the project.

Actually, only 399 of the men had syphilis; the other 201 were perfectly healthy but were included in the study as a control group. This was done so the researchers could evaluate the actual health effects of the disease by comparing medical statistics of the men with syphilis with those who were not sick. All of the participants, however, were told that they were receiving free treatment for an illness vaguely termed "bad blood." In reality, the medicine the doctors distributed to the men did nothing to alleviate the deadly illness that two-thirds of them had. By the time the story was published in 1972, at least twenty-eight of the study participants had died as a direct result of having syphilis and one hundred had died from syphilis-related conditions. In addition, forty men had infected their wives with the disease, and nineteen children had been born with congenital syphilis, which had been passed on to them by their unsuspecting parents.

The firestorm of controversy that the story ignited forced embarrassed government officials to end the research project. But when the few survivors learned the true nature of their illness, they were stunned that government officials had lied to them for so many years. As Charles Pollard explained, "They told me [in 1932] I had bad blood. All I knew was that they just kept saying I had the bad blood—they never mentioned syphilis to me, not even once."[3]

"A Case of Racial Discrimination"

The decades-long deception of the men regarding the purpose of the study and the treatment they received violated ethical standards on scientific studies involving human beings. As a result, the Tuskegee study today is considered one of the most shameful chapters in American medical history. The fact that all of the subject in the study were black contributed to the revulsion people felt when the study came to light. One of the people who were the angriest about the racial composition of the test group was Alabama attorney Fred D. Gray, who successfully sued the federal government on behalf of the study's participants. As an African American himself, Gray was shocked and enraged by the apparent racism of the scientists who designed the study:

> I saw the experiment as a case of racial discrimination and in that sense it became very personal to me, for I had dedicated my legal career to challenging the [South's racist] segregation under which the [study] participants and I were born and lived. The study was as racist as segregation in schools [because it was] conducted solely with blacks when there were also whites in the community who had syphilis.[4]

Gray, like many other people, believed that the racism that existed in America in the first half of the twentieth century heavily influenced the study. However, the doctors who began the study, originally focused on southern black men, did not do so because they were racist. They decided to study the disease among southern black men because this population had the nation's highest rate of syphilis infection and because poverty was keeping them from getting the medical attention they needed. In fact, when the study began, participants actually received minimal medical care for syphilis.

Nevertheless, when the purpose of the study was changed to researching the long-range effects of untreated syphilis, the

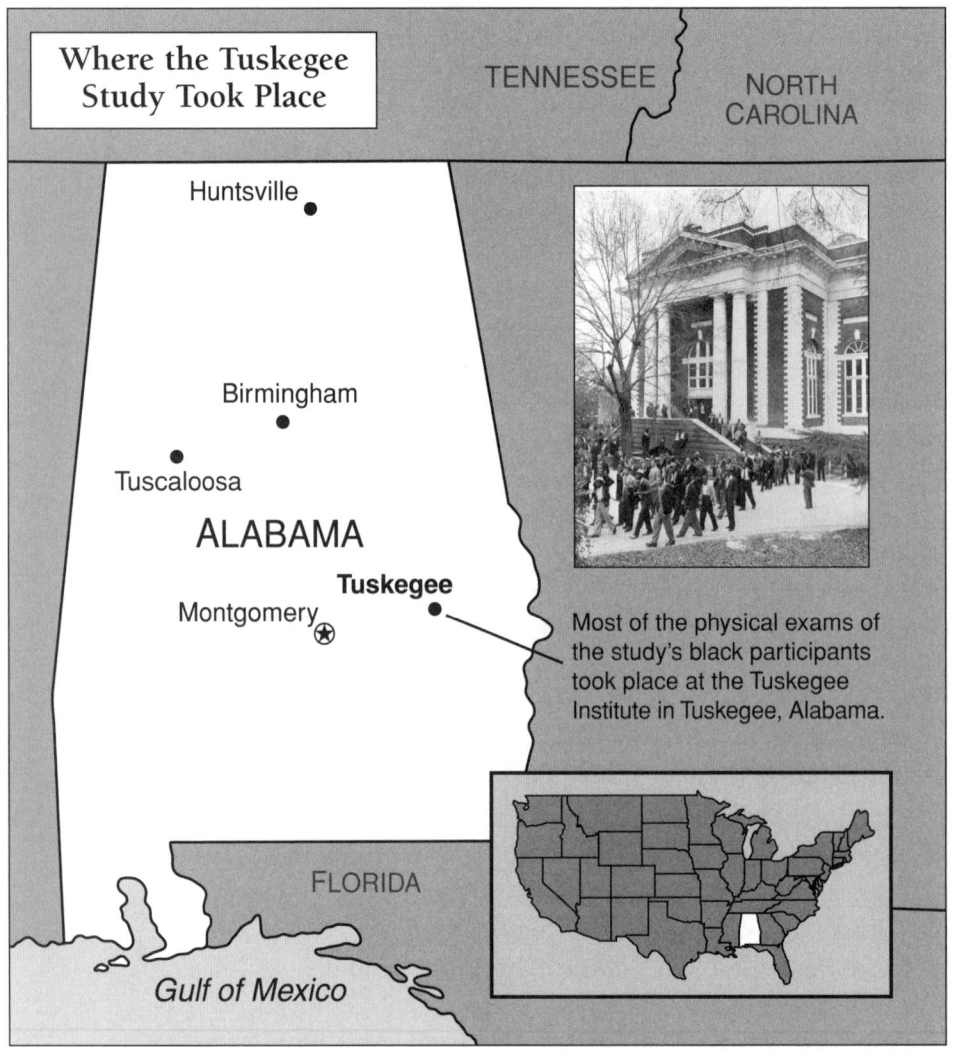

Where the Tuskegee Study Took Place

TENNESSEE

NORTH CAROLINA

Huntsville

Birmingham

Tuscaloosa

ALABAMA

Tuskegee

Montgomery

Most of the physical exams of the study's black participants took place at the Tuskegee Institute in Tuskegee, Alabama.

FLORIDA

Gulf of Mexico

treatment ended. It was at this point that many people believe racism began to play a major role in the study, one that was harmful to the men involved. In the first half of the twentieth century, many white people, including some government officials, believed that blacks were inferior to whites and that their lives therefore were not as valuable as those of whites. Gray and many other people believe that this type of racist reasoning blinded the white doctors to the ethics of denying treatment to people suffering from a deadly but treatable disease. As Gray claimed, "In my opinion, this study would never have happened to white participants."[5]

The "Shadow" of the Tuskegee Study

Dr. Vanessa Northington Gamble, a medical historian, agrees with Gray that racism made it easier for white doctors to believe it was morally acceptable to study a deadly disease's effects on black men without trying to prevent their deaths. More than a quarter century after the project was exposed, Gamble declared that the Tuskegee study "has emerged as the most prominent example of medical racism" in modern history. She also says that the facts of the research project are so stunningly brutal that "the study has moved from being a singular historical event to a powerful metaphor. It has come to symbolize racism in medicine, misconduct in human research, the arrogance of physicians, and government abuse of black people."[6]

Chapter One

Roots of the Tuskegee Study

When the Tuskegee Study of Untreated Syphilis in the Negro Male was exposed in 1972, the world learned that, for four decades, doctors paid by the U.S. government's Public Health Service had let poor black men go untreated for syphilis so that the doctors could study what the disease would do to the men's bodies. The doctors did not tell the men they had syphilis or even explain to them that they were part of a medical research study. They gave the men annual physical examinations and supplied them with what was said to be medicine to cure a condition that the doctors called "bad blood." The medicine, however, was only aspirin and vitamins, which could do nothing to alleviate the deadly effects of syphilis.

When a newspaper story finally revealed the Tuskegee study's true nature, it was quickly condemned as a terrible abuse of the rights of the men involved. Ironically, however, the study originally had never been intended to hurt the men. Instead, the program that led to the Tuskegee study had been created to reduce the suffering of southern blacks who had syphilis and prevent them from passing it on to other people.

A Test Program

The roots of the Tuskegee study lay in a health project that was initiated in the early twentieth century by Dr. Hugh S. Cumming, who at the time headed the PHS. Cumming wanted to curb the spread of the devastating disease known as syphilis, which was widespread in the United States—especially among black Americans. To find out more about the extent of the problem, Cumming conducted a survey in Bolivar County, Mississippi. The PHS examined more than two thousand African American men who worked for the Delta and Pine Land Company, a large cotton plantation, and found that about one-quarter of them had syphilis, a very high rate of infection.

Cumming wanted to help the men suffering from this crippling disease. Because his agency did not have the funds to treat them, he wrote a letter in 1929 to Michael M. Davis, the director of medical services for a charity called the Julius Rosenwald Fund. Cumming explained the findings at the Delta and Pine Land Company and requested $10,000 for a one-year test program to provide medical treatment for the men, who were too poor to pay for such care themselves. Cumming wrote: "If adequate methods of treatment can be applied among this group, it should furnish a demonstration which will be of value in connection with [helping to start]

In 1929 U.S. surgeon general Hugh S. Cumming initiated a program to stop the spread of syphilis among poor southern blacks.

The Disease Syphilis

—————————■—————————

People still get syphilis, a sexually transmitted disease caused by a bacterium called *Treponema pallidum*. But because syphilis today can be cured with penicillin, it is no longer as feared as it once was. The following information on this disease is from an Internet medical encyclopedia available through the U.S. National Library of Medicine and National Institutes of Health:

> Syphilis has several stages. In the primary stage, painless sores, called chancres, appear approximately 2 to 3 weeks after initial exposure. Some individuals with primary syphilis may not notice chancres nor have symptoms associated with them. In about 4 to 6 weeks chancres will usually disappear. Approximately one-third of untreated individuals will progress to the second stage: secondary syphilis. This usually occurs at about 2 to 8 weeks after the appearance of the original chancre; in some cases the chancre may still be present. Secondary syphilis is the stage where the bacteria have spread in the bloodstream and have reached their highest numbers. The most common symptoms include:

similar programs in other localities and industries in which there is a high prevalence of syphilis."[7]

It was natural for Cumming to make such an appeal to the Rosenwald Fund. This philanthropic organization sought to help poor blacks in a variety of ways. For example, the fund built schools in the South that black children could attend. At the time, blacks were not allowed to go to most schools with whites, and the public schools for blacks were substandard. Because another of the fund's goals was to improve medical care for blacks, it agreed to financially assist the PHS in treating the plantation workers. The Delta and Pine Land Company also agreed to help; the company and the Rosenwald Fund each contributed $10,000 to the project.

Dr. Oliver C. Wenger, director of the PHS Venereal Disease Clinic in Hot Springs, Arkansas, was chosen to oversee the test skin rash which can be varied in appearance, yet frequently involves the palms and soles, in addition to lesions in the mouth [and genital areas], swollen lymph nodes, and fever. This stage is the most contagious stage of syphilis. It usually resolves within weeks to a year. A latent phase follows, which may last for years and is characterized by the absence of symptoms. The final stage of syphilis is called tertiary syphilis [and it occurs] 3 to 15 years after the infection.

The encyclopedia notes that it is in that final stage that a patient suffers the most severe health effects, such as heart disease, brain damage, insanity, and a variety of other physical problems, many of which lead to death.

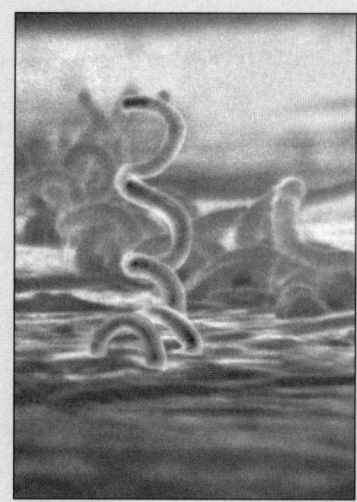

The bacterium *Treponema pallidum*, shown in this electron micrograph, is responsible for syphilis.

program. Wenger gave each of the nearly five hundred patients twenty-five injections of neoarsphenamine, a drug containing arsenic, which is toxic to many organisms, including the bacterium that causes syphilis. He also supplied patients with an ointment containing mercury, which they were told to rub on areas of their lower body where the disease had caused open sores. Arsenic and mercury are also toxic to human beings in large doses; some patients experienced negative side effects from such treatments, including high fevers and damage to the heart. Although the side effects were undesirable, the treatment Wenger prescribed was the best available at the time.

The treatment was not just unpleasant; it was expensive, and funds were limited. The PHS, therefore, could afford to provide care for patients for just a few weeks, a period that was far short of the nearly yearlong series of treatments considered necessary to cure syphilis. In a letter to Davis on August 13, 1929, Wenger said that he was treating blacks "not in the hope of effecting a cure but to make as many of these patients noninfectious"[8] as he could, which meant they could no longer transmit the disease to others.

Despite the limited duration of the treatments, the health of many patients improved. The resident manager of the Delta and Pine Land Company was pleased because his workers were healthier and thus more productive. Admitting to Wenger that for him the health of black workers was basically "a matter of dollars and cents," the manager said: "As a result [of the program], I never had so little sickness as last year. This is the best thing we have ever done. See that old man over there? Last year he could hardly drag himself around, sores all over his legs, cripp[l]ed up with rheumatism; now he does as good a day's work as any man on the place."[9]

Syphilis and the Black Population

Because the test program in Mississippi had been so successful, the PHS and the Rosenwald Fund decided to begin another, much larger study of syphilis among southern blacks. In November 1929 the Rosenwald Fund gave the PHS $50,000 to pay for what were called syphilis control projects in six southern states. The project sites were in Macon County, Alabama; Glynn County, Georgia; Bolivar County, Mississippi, the site of the original program; Pitt County, North Carolina; Tipton County, Tennessee; and Albemarle County, Virginia. The sites were spread across the South to provide a wide-ranging look at rates of syphilis in blacks.

Through these studies and others, the PHS discovered that syphilis was a major health problem for rural blacks such as those who worked for the Delta and Pine Land Company. The PHS found an average of about five syphilis cases for every 1,000 people. The rate of syphilis for whites was about four per thousand while that of blacks was about seven per thousand. Another PHS survey showed that the rate of infection among blacks was generally double that of the white population.

There were several theories as to why blacks had higher rates of syphilis than whites. One was that blacks suffered higher rates of syphilis because they were physically, morally, and mentally inferior to whites. According to this racist view, blacks were not as physically advanced as whites, which made blacks more susceptible to disease. White racists also considered blacks more sexually promiscuous, which proved that they were morally inferior. Racist beliefs about blacks were summed up in 1903 by Dr. W.T. English, who wrote in a Georgia medical journal that "the body of the negro [is] a mass of minor defects and imperfections from the crown of the head to the soles of the feet."[10]

Racists even claimed that the higher rates of syphilis infection proved that blacks were less intelligent than whites since it showed that blacks did not bother to take precautions against catching such a terrible disease. As late as 1932, one doctor stated that the

Residents of a small Georgia town are tested for syphilis at a clinic in 1935. The number of syphilis cases among blacks was nearly double that of whites at the time.

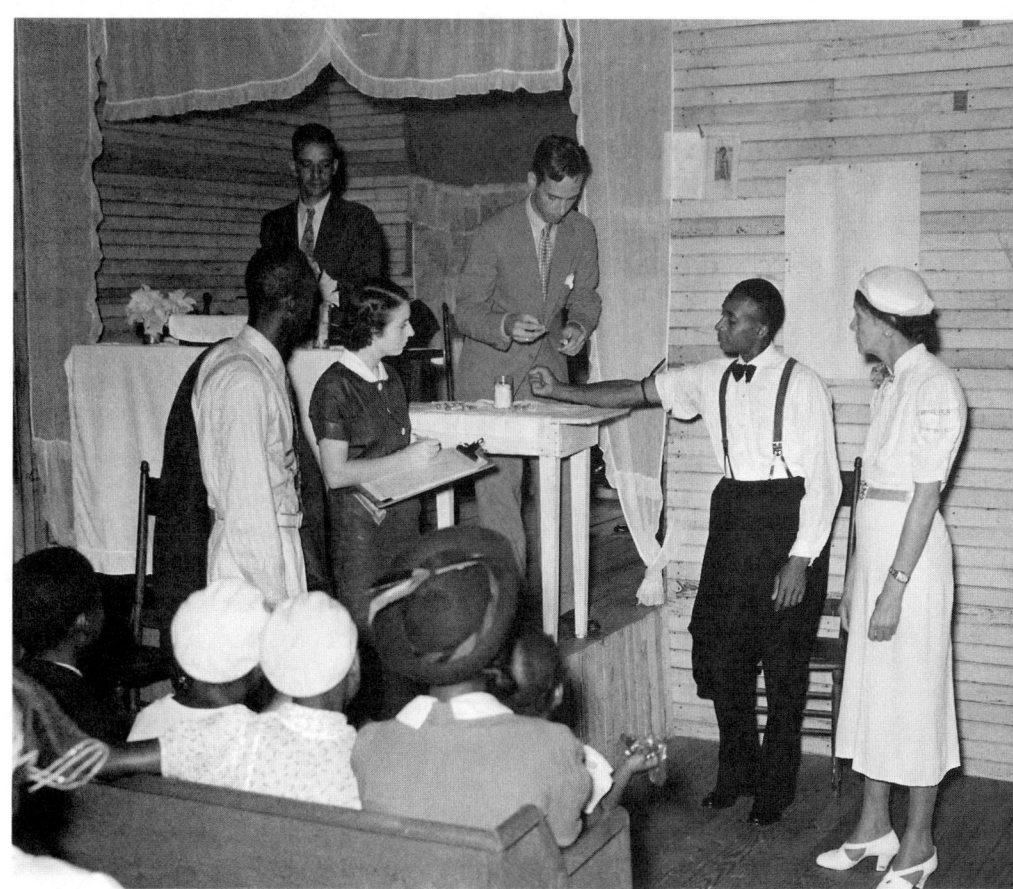

difference in the rates of syphilis was "partly a reflection of the greater interest of the white race in its health."[11] According to author Andrew Goliszek, "Racial medicine, as such theories were called, perpetuated the myth that blacks had lower immunity,

Shadow on the Land

The doctors who initiated the Tuskegee study were more liberal in their views about blacks and syphilis than were most physicians during the period. Instead of believing that blacks suffered higher rates of the disease than whites did because blacks were inferior, physicians like Dr. Thomas Parran realized that this difference was due to social and economic factors. In his 1937 book *Shadow on the Land: Syphilis, the White Man's Burden*, Parran notes that it was whites who introduced syphilis to blacks and that the main factors contributing to higher rates of infection among blacks were social:

> It has been said that the negro slave brought to America malaria and hookworm disease. If he did, the white man paid him back by giving him tuberculosis and syphilis. The fact that he is at the bottom of the economic ladder contributed to his abnormally high [syphilis] rate. For among the third of our population which is ill fed, ill clothed, and ill housed, as a race, north and south, and especially in the rural south, his house is the most miserable, his clothing the scantiest, and his food ration the most poorly balanced.

Dr. Thomas Parran concluded that the high incidence of syphilis among blacks was a direct result of social and economic factors.

greater susceptibility to disease, and self-destructive behaviors that led to a decline in health."[12]

Slowly, however, many doctors and medical researchers in the early twentieth century had been abandoning such explicitly racist ideas. They were beginning to believe that social factors such as personal income, education, and availability of medical care were more important than race in determining the incidence of many diseases, including syphilis.

Among this group of new thinkers was Dr. Thomas Parran of the PHS. In his 1937 book about syphilis, *Shadow on the Land*, Parran rejected racist attitudes and claimed that social factors most directly affected disease rates. He argued that people of either race who were educated would know about the dangers of a disease like syphilis and would be likely to take precautions against catching it. Parran also said that people who could afford medical care when they became ill, regardless of their race, had lower rates of disease. Parran concluded: "Wherever education and living conditions among the negro race approximate that of the white race, the syphilis rate approximates that of the white."[13]

Parran cited research he had done that he claimed proved that social and economic conditions affected disease rates. He had studied students at Meharry Medical College in Nashville, Tennessee, a black medical school whose students came from families with more education and money than most blacks of the period had. According to Parran, the rate of syphilis infection among those students was far lower than the rate among poor blacks.

Effects of Racism

Parran cited enduring social conditions as the real reason for higher rates of syphilis among blacks. In the first half of the twentieth century, blacks were denied many of their basic civil rights. Racism was strongest in southern states, where laws known as Jim Crow strictly segregated blacks and whites. These discriminatory laws determined where blacks could live, eat, shop, attend school, and even drink from a public water fountain or use a public restroom. Blacks were also denied the right to vote in elections, which meant they had no opportunity to gain political power so they could stop the discrimination.

Racial discrimination generally denied blacks a chance to obtain a decent education or learn skills that would prepare them to hold high-paying jobs. Thus, most blacks were relegated to a life of poverty because they were allowed to hold only the most menial and low-paying positions. But even when blacks had the education and skills to work as mechanics, lawyers, or journalists, racist whites usually refused to hire them. In the South, where segregation was most rigorously enforced, most blacks had little choice of occupation. They either did menial labor or became sharecroppers, tenant farmers who grew crops on land they rented from whites.

Macon County, Alabama

The conditions in Macon County, Alabama, which would become the site of the Tuskegee study, were typical of the way blacks lived in the rural South in this period. Macon County was part of Alabama's "black belt," a name derived from both the region's rich, dark soil and its high percentage of black citizens. Macon County in 1930 had 27,103 residents, and 22,230 of them were black. In *Reaping the Whirlwind: The Civil Rights Movement in Tuskegee*, author Robert J. Norrell explains how poverty affected their lives:

> Health conditions for rural blacks in Macon County were miserable, generally. Their diet consisted largely of salt pork, hominy grits [cornmeal], cornbread, and molasses; fresh meat, breads, vegetables, fruit, and milk were rarely included. Malnutrition was chronic, and they were afflicted by many diet-related illnesses. Most of the county's poor blacks could not afford medical care.[14]

Most Macon County blacks lived in crude wooden shacks that had dirt floors, little furniture, and no indoor plumbing. Their water for drinking, cooking, and bathing came from outdoor wells, which were often contaminated by various forms of pollution. Macon County blacks were also poorly educated. A 1932 study showed that 227 out of every 1,000 blacks there were illiterate, an illiteracy rate nearly ten times that of local whites.

Most southern blacks at the time of the Tuskegee study lived in crude wooden shacks that lacked indoor plumbing, like this one in rural Georgia.

A New Project

This was the picture in Macon County when, as part of the six-county syphilis control project started the previous year, PHS workers in 1930 began going door to door to ask volunteers to take blood tests for syphilis. When the PHS had trouble getting people to volunteer for the study, it recruited black leaders to host informational meetings in churches and schools. Black ministers, teachers, nurses, and doctors attended these meetings. The presence of these trusted, respected members of the black community assured the volunteers that the tests would not harm them. The doctors and nurses then took blood samples from the volunteers, either at the meeting or afterward. Blood was drawn from each person with a needle and examined under a microscope to see if the bacteria that cause syphilis were present. The blood samples were taken from men and women of all ages as well as from children, since children can be born with the disease if their mother has it. Parran describes the scene:

> After the talk came the call for testing. Sometimes it was done on the spot, blood specimens taken from everybody in the place. Usually it was not difficult to get blood specimens from the whole crowd, once a leader among them had been persuaded to submit to the first test. When testing was done at a school session, a lollypop apiece helped to motivate the timid small fry [children].[15]

Bad Blood

In asking the black residents of Macon County to submit to the tests, government doctors said they were trying to find out if they had "bad blood." Parran explained that doctors used that term because they thought that uneducated blacks would not know the disease's proper medical name: "Though most of the audience did not know the word syphilis, many of them were familiar with what they called 'bad-blood' disease and the miseries it brought."[16]

Although Parran and other doctors believed that the people being asked would understand that "bad blood" referred to the symptoms associated with syphilis, they were mistaken. The phrase was a vague way of referring to a host of physical ailments—headaches, indigestion, sores on their bodies, sterility, and even a general feeling that they were run down physically. The term was used by almost everyone who felt sick. Thus, the people who volunteered did not realize that the illness they were being tested for was syphilis, a disease that could have severe physical consequences and could even kill them. This misunderstanding actually made it easier for the PHS to round up people to test because they thought they were being tested for a variety of ailments they associated with "bad blood."

So it was that in 1930 the PHS collected blood samples from forty thousand blacks. Test results showed that across the six counties being studied, approximately 25 percent of the individuals had syphilis. The lowest rate was 7 percent in Albemarle County, where blacks were generally more educated and had better-paying jobs than those in the other five test sites. The highest rate of infection was 36 percent, in Macon County.

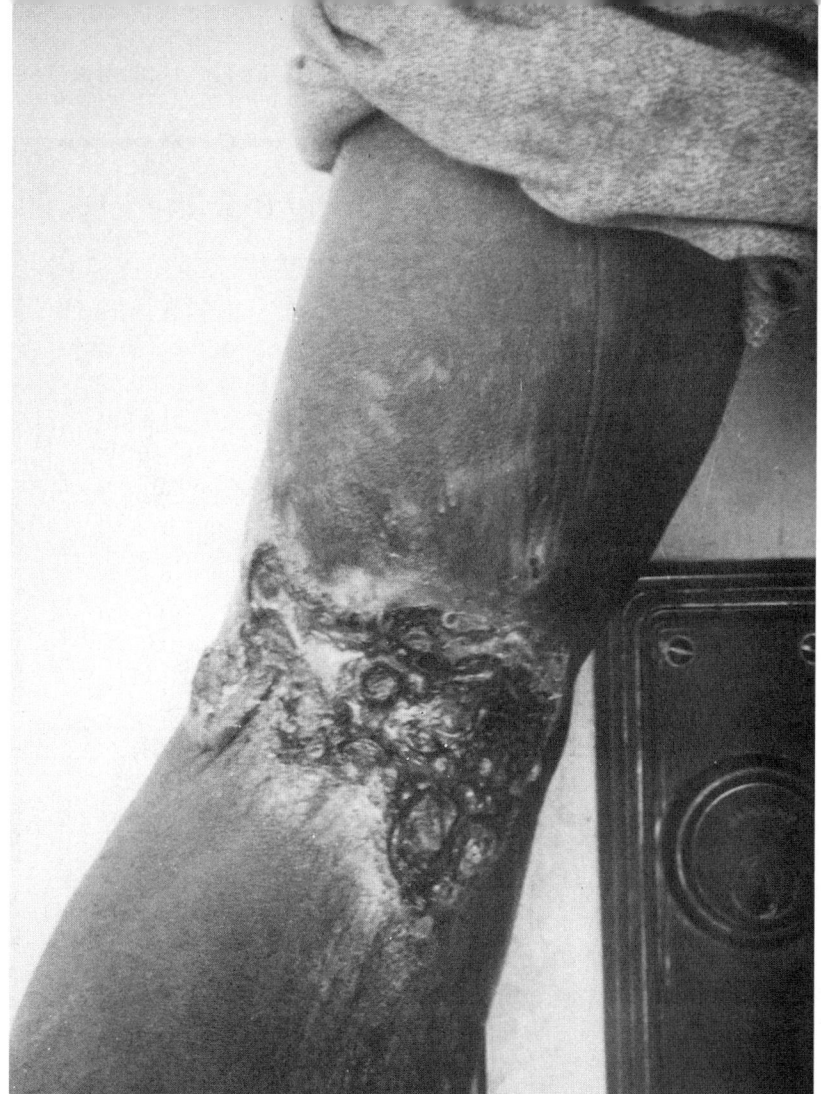

Syphilis has eaten away the skin of this study participant. Despite such horrific symptoms, participants in the 1930 PHS syphilis study were not treated for the disease.

Treating Syphilis

Like the Delta and Pine Land Company workers in the 1929 program, test subjects in Macon County who were diagnosed with syphilis were given neoarsphenamine shots and supplies of mercury ointment. To be effective, the mercury ointment had to be rubbed thoroughly into the patient's skin so that it could be absorbed into the bloodstream. To ensure this was done properly, patients were told to smear the ointment inside their socks; the resulting rubbing motion when they walked during the day would help their bodies absorb the medicine.

Medical Studies Using Blacks

Vanessa Northington Gamble, an African American medical historian, argues that the Tuskegee study was not the first time the medical profession had abused the rights of black Americans in medical studies. In her article "Under the Shadow of Tuskegee: African Americans and Health Care," Gamble explains that black slaves were often forced to be subjects of medical experiments:

> Although physicians also used poor Whites as subjects, they used Black people far more often. During an 1835 trip to the United States, French visitor Harriet Martineau found that Black people lacked the power even to protect the graves of their dead. "In Baltimore the bodies of coloured people exclusively are taken for dissection," she remarked, "because the Whites do not like it, and the coloured people cannot resist." Four years later, abolitionist Theodore Dwight Weld echoed Martineau's sentiment. "Public opinion," he wrote, "would tolerate surgical experiments, operations, processes, performed upon them [slaves], which it would [condemn] if performed upon their master or other whites." Slaves found themselves as subjects of medical experiments . . . because the state considered them property and denied them the legal right to refuse to participate.

Because many rural blacks often went barefoot, however, another way had to be found to make sure the mercury would be continuously rubbed in to the patient's skin. PHS officials gave the patients rubber and canvas belts, which they covered with the medicinal ointment and wore all day. The constant rubbing of the belt against their skin helped the medicine to be absorbed into their bodies. Parran describes the instructions that doctors gave patients: "Take this package of salve [ointment], cut it into six pieces. Every morning, smear one piece on the belt, like this [the doctor would show them how to do that]. Tie the belt tightly around your waist; on the seventh day, wash yourself thoroughly and meet me here. Don't forget, one week from today."[17]

As in the 1929 syphilis control program, the amount of treatment given to the patients was only enough to weaken the disease and make them noninfectious. Neither the Rosenwald Fund, the PHS, nor state health agencies that were also involved in the program had enough money to give patients the standard full course of treatment to eliminate syphilis, which could require sixty visits to a doctor and take up to a year. And even that many treatments did not always cure the disease.

A "Useless . . . Attempt to Cure Syphilis"

In the spring of 1930 the Rosenwald Fund sent Dr. H.L. Harris Jr., a black physician, to Macon County to assess the effectiveness of the syphilis control project. In a report to Dr. Davis, who headed the Rosenwald Fund's medical programs, Harris criticized the way the program was being run. Harris wrote that doctors and nurses were overworked, operated in deteriorating schools and other substandard buildings, and had limited medical equipment.

Still, although such conditions made it difficult to diagnose patients properly and treat them effectively, Harris believed the program was accomplishing some good by highlighting the huge syphilis problem in Macon County. He wrote, "To the extent that the demonstration has caused county, state and federal authorities to take an interest in health problems of a very backward Negro community, the effort is very much worthwhile."[18]

Harris visited Macon County again in September 1930. In a second report to Davis, Harris said that 3,684 Wassermann tests, which reveal the presence of syphilis antibodies in blood, had been performed. Thirty-six percent of them were positive, indicating the person had syphilis. Harris noted that 1,271 patients with syphilis had already begun receiving treatment in six Macon County clinics.

However, Harris now began to doubt that the project was significantly improving the health of local blacks. He reasoned that they suffered from so many illnesses that treating just one disease was not enough to alter their overall health. In his report, Harris wrote that Macon County blacks needed a comprehensive program that could meet all their medical needs: "It is useless to attempt to cure syphilis in the rural Negro population until and unless some way is found to treat the large number of cases of tuberculosis, malnutrition and pellagra [a condition caused by poor diet], and also to give [poor blacks] some fundamental training in [healthy] living habits."[19]

Claiming that the project had done all it could to help Macon County blacks, Harris recommended that the Rosenwald Fund end its participation. In April 1931 Davis appointed Parran and Dr. A.L. Keyes, an expert on syphilis, to review the syphilis projects that the Rosenwald Fund was financing.

Funding Withdrawn

In a report delivered in May 1932, Parran and Keyes praised the projects for helping to control syphilis and contributing to knowledge of the disease's prevalence among rural blacks. However, their glowing words were unable to save the programs. Despite the success of the programs in improving the health of poor blacks, the Rosenwald Fund trustees voted to discontinue funding for the syphilis control demonstrations. The reason the trustees withdrew their support was the Great Depression. The financial downturn, which had begun in 1929, had left the organization without adequate funds to continue financing such projects.

PHS officials who had participated in the control project were upset about the decision because they believed they were learning valuable new facts about syphilis. Their desire to acquire even more knowledge about this deadly disease would soon lead them to begin the Tuskegee Study of Untreated Syphilis in the Negro Male.

Chapter Two

The Tuskegee Study Is Born

After the Rosenwald Fund withdrew its financial support from the syphilis control projects, Dr. Taliaferro Clark, an assistant surgeon general with the U.S. Public Health Service, began working on a final report to summarize what the programs had accomplished. Clark was disappointed that the projects were ending. He believed they had done a lot of good; they had increased knowledge of the problem syphilis posed among blacks and had resulted in many people who had the disease being treated.

While reviewing data that had been collected in the six counties, Clark was struck by the fact that, of the fourteen hundred Macon County patients who had been treated, only thirty-three had ever had any previous medical care for syphilis. Those statistics made Clark think that even if the PHS did not have enough money to *treat* people in Macon County infected with syphilis, it could still continue *studying* the individuals there who had the deadly disease. As Clark wrote to a colleague in September 1932, "The thought came to me that the Alabama community offered an unparalleled opportunity for the study of untreated syphilis."[20]

Why Study Untreated Syphilis in Blacks?

Clark decided to focus the study of the long-term effects of syphilis on African Americans because no one had ever researched how this disease developed over many years in that population. The only previous study of untreated syphilis had been done with a large group of white men in Norway in the late nineteenth century.

Left untreated, syphilis does not have serious health effects until three to fifteen years after a person is infected. The initial effects of syphilis are uncomfortable but not life threatening.

The Tuskegee study was the brainchild of Taliaferro Clark, an assistant surgeon general, who devised the study as a means to assess the long-term effects of syphilis.

They include open sores on the genitals and a skin rash, symptoms that disappear after a few months. However, the bacterium that causes syphilis can remain in a person's body and after several years begin causing a variety of severe medical problems, such as heart disease, blindness, and insanity. Left untreated, syphilis is eventually fatal.

Although there was no statistical proof, scientists believed that syphilis ran its course differently in blacks and whites. At the time, whites were thought to have more neurosyphilis symptoms while blacks were thought to have more cardiovascular problems. Although the same bacterium is responsible, neurosyphilis attacks the brain, while cardiovascular syphilis attacks the heart. The theory that blacks would suffer less neurosyphilis than whites stemmed from racist beliefs that blacks were intellectually inferior to whites and thus would not develop brain damage. Dr. Joseph Earle Moore of the Venereal Disease Clinic of the Johns Hopkins University School of Medicine even went so far as to claim, "Syphilis in the Negro is in many respects almost a different disease from syphilis in the white."[21] Clark, who knew about the past research in Norway involving whites, saw an opportunity to find out if there were, in fact, any differences in how syphilis affected the two races.

Those were the factors that led Clark to decide to study untreated syphilis in blacks. Clark then chose Macon County as the site of the study for two important reasons. The first was that the county had a large number of potential research subjects: Macon County's blacks had had the highest rate of infection in the six southern counties surveyed in 1930 as well as a very low rate of treatment. The second reason for Clark's decision was the presence of the Tuskegee Institute's John A. Andrew Memorial Hospital. It was one of the few medical facilities in the racially segregated South that admitted blacks, which meant the test subjects could receive the extensive physical examinations needed for the research.

The Tuskegee Study

It was in this way that the Tuskegee Study of Untreated Syphilis in the Negro Male was born. Before the study could begin, however, Clark needed to secure permission from state officials and the Tuskegee Institute to do the research.

In a letter dated August 29, 1932, Clark presented his proposal for what was to become the Tuskegee study to Dr. J.N. Baker, the Alabama state health officer. Clark said that the PHS wanted to examine men who had had syphilis for at least five years so that it could assess the disease's long-term effects. He said the study would last only between six months and a year, depending on how long it took to gather the data.

In mid-September Clark and Dr. Wenger, who still headed the PHS Venereal Disease Clinic in Hot Springs, Arkansas, traveled to Montgomery, Alabama, to meet with Alabama health officials. The state and local officials approved the project, but only after making Clark promise to provide at least minimal treatment to people who were found to have syphilis.

On September 30, Surgeon General Cumming, the PHS's top official, wrote to Dr. Robert R. Moton of the Tuskegee Institute to secure his support for the project. Describing the study in glowing terms as "an unparalleled opportunity for carrying on this piece of scientific research which probably cannot be duplicated anywhere else in the world," Cumming stressed that because hospital facilities were needed to examine patients, "the success of this important study really hinges on your cooperation."[22]

Moton gave his consent a few days later, as did the Alabama State Board of Health and the Macon County Board of Health. The Tuskegee Study of Untreated Syphilis in the Negro Male could now begin.

Recruiting Participants

Clark had been so confident that Moton and the heads of the other agencies would cooperate that he had already begun organizing the study by making two key personnel appointments. Clark named Dr. Raymond H. Vonderlehr of the PHS as the study's on-site director. Clark also hired a black nurse named Eunice Rivers, who had trained at Tuskegee's hospital and was now its supervisor of night nurses. In the years to come, Rivers would emerge as one of the study's key figures because of the strong personal relationships she forged with its participants.

Vonderlehr arrived in Tuskegee on October 19, 1932. PHS personnel once again held meetings in schools and churches to take blood samples from people. When no building was avail-

Ignorance of Syphilis

The blacks of Macon County had little real knowledge about syphilis and were not even aware that it was transmitted sexually. In his 1934 book, *The Shadow of the Plantation*, Charles Johnson discusses this lack of knowledge. The following excerpt from his book is from *Tuskegee's Truths: Rethinking the Tuskegee Syphilis Study*, edited by Susan M. Reverby:

> In the entire 612 families interviewed there was not a single expression which seemed to connect syphilis with the sexual act. The fact of "bad blood" carried little social stigma and was spoken of in about the same manner as one speaks of having a "bad heart" or "bad teeth." In but few instances was "bad blood" associated with syphilis as a venereal disease. Where there were obvious physical manifestations of the disease the persons were referred to as being afflicted, but this was generalized. Often no distinction was made between complaints and the symptoms of "bad blood." Accordingly, treatments for bad blood were expected to cure headaches, indigestion, pellagra, sterility, sores of various sorts, and general run-down conditions.

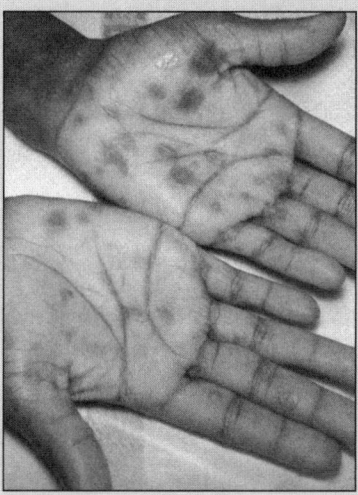

Most blacks in Macon County were ignorant of the symptoms of syphilis, which include skin eruptions like these.

able, doctors sometimes met with people under the shade of a large tree. Once again, Macon County blacks were told they were being tested for "bad blood," not syphilis. Dr. J.W. Williams, who was studying at John A. Andrew Memorial Hospital in 1932,

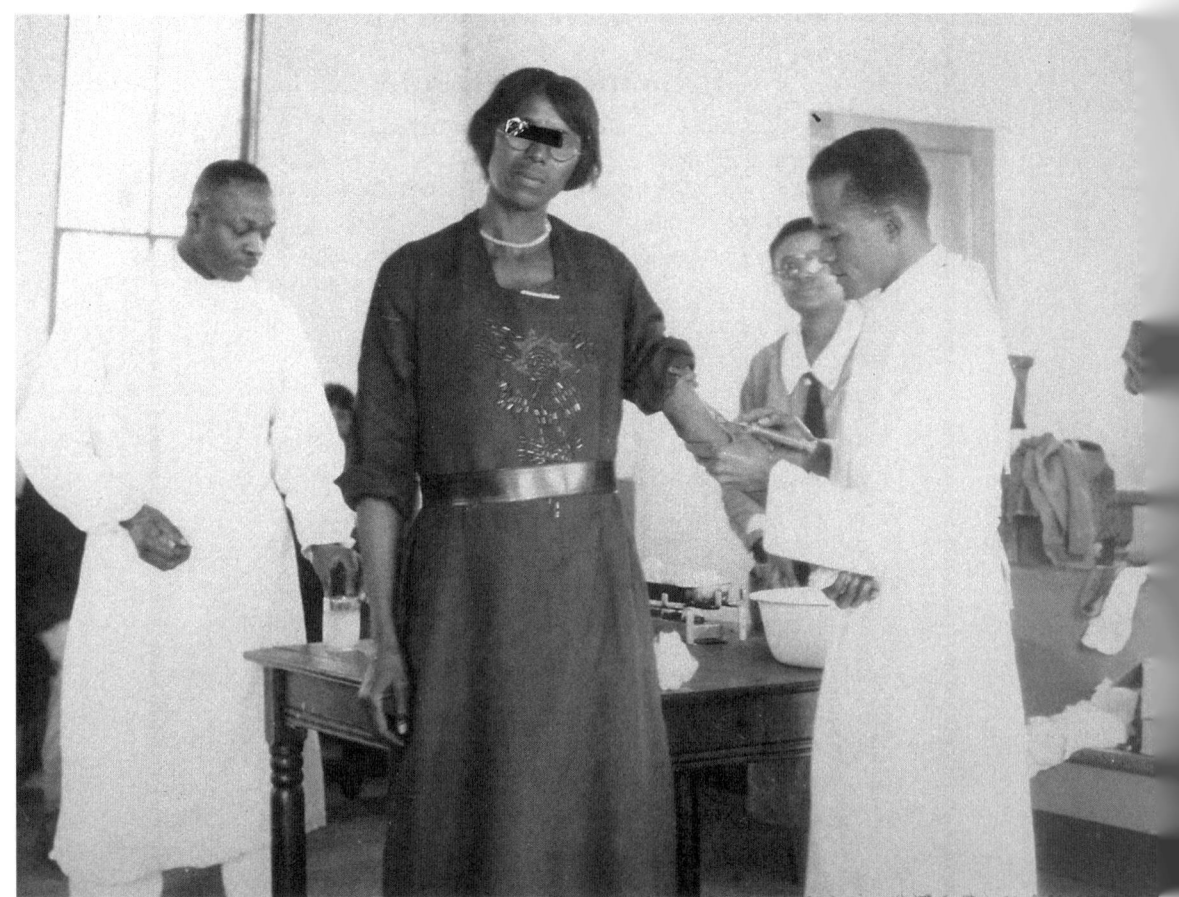

An unidentified woman is tested for syphilis. Women were tested in order to allay fears that the Tuskegee study was merely a ploy to lure black men into the armed forces.

helped examine candidates for inclusion in the study. He later admitted that the men were never told about the true nature of their illness or that they were being tested as part of a medical study about the long-term effects of syphilis:

> The people who came in were not told what was being done. We told them we wanted to test them. They were not told, so far as I know, what they were being treated for or what they were not being treated for. [The subjects] thought they were being treated for rheumatism or bad stomachs. We didn't tell them we were looking for syphilis. I don't think they would have known what that was.[23]

Syphilis Testing

Each day for several weeks, Wenger, Vonderlehr, and one or two black interns from Andrew Hospital traveled to six or seven sites in Macon County to draw blood from potential participants. In the first week they collected three hundred samples, which were sent to the state health laboratory for testing to see if the person had syphilis.

People who tested positive for syphilis became candidates for inclusion in the study. Because the symptoms of syphilis in its more advanced stages do not appear until about five years after someone has been infected, the PHS needed to know how long a person had had the disease. It is harder for doctors to know when women first contracted syphilis because the disease's early symptoms are less obvious in women than in men. For that reason, the PHS limited its pool of candidates to men. And because older subjects were likely to have more advanced cases of syphilis, the PHS also decided that participants should be at least twenty-five years old.

Even though PHS doctors wanted only men for the study, they also tested women in the early selection process. Officials thought that if they examined only men over the age of twenty-five, no men would show up because they would fear they were being examined in preparation for induction into the nation's armed forces. This had happened to many local blacks fifteen years earlier during World War I. Since women at the time were not allowed to serve in the military, the PHS thought that testing both men and women would allay fears that the blood test was actually a trick to lure black men into the army.

Men with positive test results who were considered suitable subjects for the study were brought to Andrew Hospital for extensive physical examinations. In addition to a second blood test to confirm they had syphilis, the men were required to give doctors a detailed personal medical history, have chest X-rays and electrocardiograms administered to check for heart damage, and undergo other tests that could evaluate their health and assess any damage that syphilis had already caused.

Some Received Treatment

At the same time that the PHS was choosing a pool of candidates to include in the study, it was also treating men and women who had syphilis. The agency did this to honor the promise it had made to Alabama officials in order to win their permission to conduct the study. Clark had not wanted to treat anyone because his agency did not have much money to pay for such treatment. He had agreed to the demand only because the proposed study was supposed to last only a few months and would not entail a long-term treatment commitment.

The PHS decided to give people who were found to have syphilis eight doses of neoarsphenamine as well as a supply of mercury ointment. This level of treatment was considered far short of what was needed to cure syphilis, but officials hoped it would be enough to render the patients noninfectious. Everyone who tested positive for syphilis, including men who would ultimately be chosen as participants in the Tuskegee study, was supposed to receive this minimal treatment.

By January 1, 1933, the PHS was operating six clinics and treating five hundred patients a week. Although some people did not receive even the minimal amount of treatment Clark had approved because doctors kept running out of medicine, the cost of caring for so many people was high and Clark complained to Vonderlehr about the mounting bills. In a January 22 letter, Vonderlehr defended the money being spent: "Expenditure of several hundred dollars for drugs for these men would be well worth while if their interest and cooperation would be maintained in doing so."[24]

It took Vonderlehr until February 1933 to choose 407 black men with syphilis as potential subjects for the Tuskegee study. He then gave them a new blood test to find out if the minimal treatment they had received was curing them. He discovered that very few were being cured: Only 3 percent of those who had tested positive now seemed to be free of the disease.

Spinal Taps

A final pool of 370 candidates was at last chosen to be part of the Tuskegee Study of Untreated Syphilis in the Negro Male. Now, Vonderlehr had to perform a medical test on the men to determine which of them had neurosyphilis. Because neurosyphilis affects the brain, often in subtle ways, such as through memory loss or emotional problems, it was difficult to know who was suffering that type of damage from the disease. Only a spinal tap

A Deceitful Invitation

———————■———————

In April 1933, when doctors for the U.S. Public Health Service wanted to get nearly four hundred men with syphilis to undergo painful spinal taps, they sent them a letter that lied about the procedure. The following text of the letter is from *In the Name of Science*, by Andrew Goliszek:

Dear Sir:

Some time ago you were given a thorough examination and since that time we hope you have gotten a great deal of treatment for bad blood. You will now be given your last chance to get a second examination. This examination is a very special one, and after it is finished you will be given a special treatment [the spinal tap] if it is believed you are in a condition to stand it. . . . You will remember that you had to wait for some time when you had your last good examination, and we wish to let you know that because we expect to be so busy it may be necessary for you to remain in the hospital over one night. If this is necessary you will be furnished your meal and a bed, as well as the examination and treatment without cost.

REMEMBER, THIS IS YOUR LAST CHANCE FOR A SPECIAL FREE TREATMENT.

could prove conclusively which men had neurosyphilis, and that proof was key to the experiment's goal of finding out if the disease affected blacks and whites differently. The PHS researchers would then compare their findings with those from the study conducted in Norway decades earlier.

To perform a spinal tap, doctors insert a large needle into the base of the spine and remove spinal fluid. A spinal tap can be very painful, as well as dangerous: Patients who had spinal taps in this era often suffered severe headaches for days or weeks, numbness or stiffness of the limbs, and temporary or even permanent paralysis.

In late April, Vonderlehr sent men who had tested positive for syphilis a letter asking them to visit Andrew Hospital. To entice the men to have the spinal tap, he deliberately misled them about the procedure. He said he was offering them a chance to receive a "very special" examination and "a special treatment" for their "bad blood," one that would improve their health.[25] Clark, his superior, knew about the deception. Clark later defended the ruse by claiming, "These negroes are very ignorant and easily influenced by things that would be of minor significance in a more intelligent group."[26]

A Tuskegee study subject undergoes a spinal tap to obtain spinal fluid for neurosyphilis testing. The subjects were duped into agreeing to the painful and dangerous procedure.

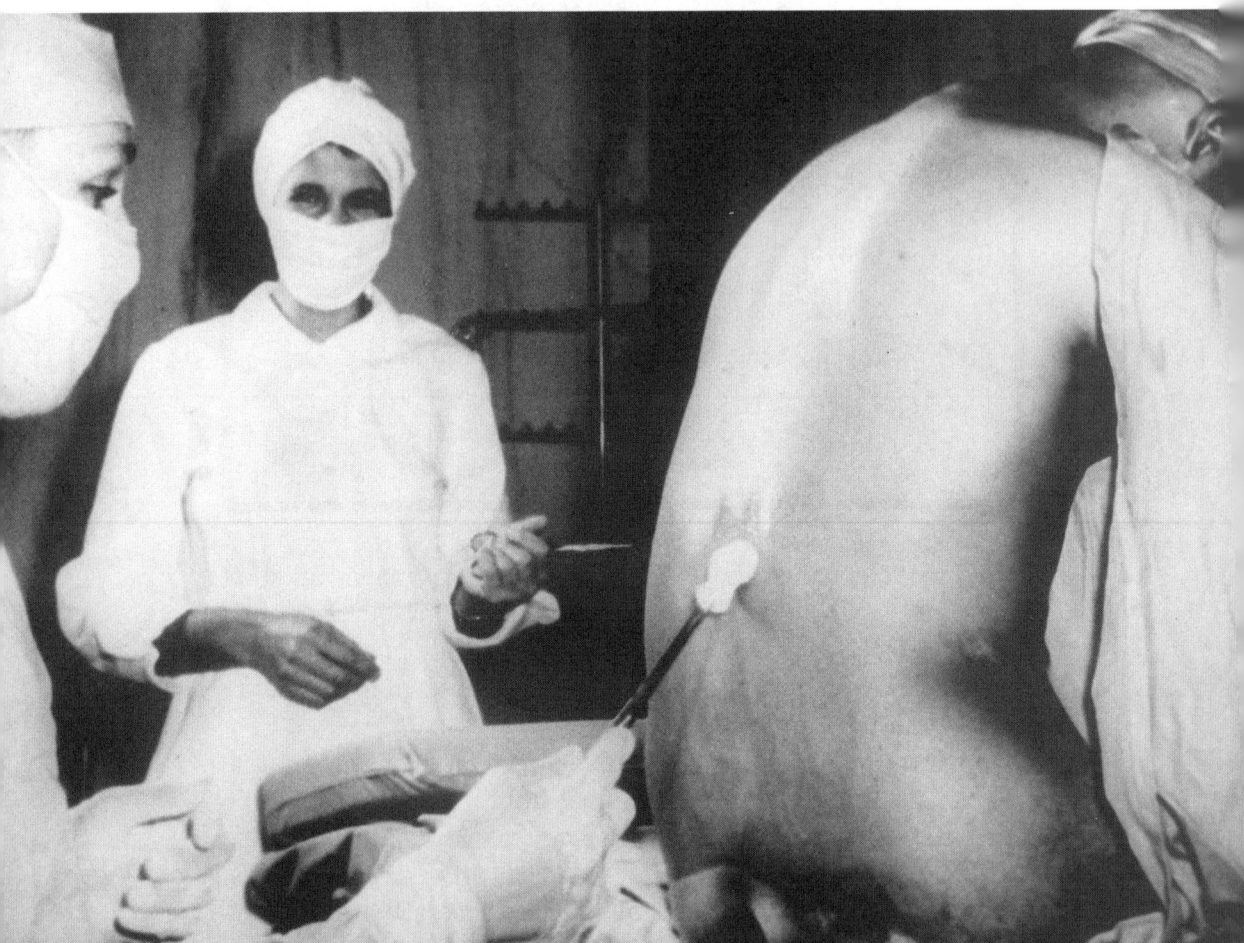

Like the other men who received the invitation, Ernest Hendon was deceived into believing that the spinal tap was a special medical treatment. "They give me a test in the back and they draw something out of me. They said it would do you good,"[27] he reported many years later.

This "special treatment," however, did not benefit the men's health. Instead, it was excruciatingly painful and left many of the men with harmful side effects. "It knocked me out," said one man. "I tell you I thought I wasn't going to make it. I fainted, you know. Just paralyzed for a day or two. Just couldn't do nothing."[28] For weeks afterward many of the men had headaches, muscular pains and spasms, and even partial paralysis. At least one man claimed he suffered recurring headaches for the rest of his life, something that doctors know is a possible side effect of a spinal tap.

Decades later when the public learned about the Tuskegee study, many people were surprised that it had been so easy for doctors to trick the men into believing they had "bad blood" and to make them undergo such painful procedures as spinal taps. Attorney Fred D. Gray claims this happened because the social and economic conditions that African Americans had to endure in this period created a strong psychological effect on the men. Said Gray, who as a black man had encountered racism while growing up in Alabama:

> The men who were chosen as participants for this study came out of the cotton cultures of the 1930s. They were for the most part very poor, not well educated [and] were by custom and social conditions accustomed to submitting to [white] authority and uniforms, whether that uniform was that of the law or the white coats and dresses of doctors and nurses.[29]

In the white-dominated South of the 1930s, blacks were accustomed to doing what they were told by whites. This culture of subservience made it easier for PHS doctors to make vulnerable men into unknowing participants in the Tuskegee study.

The PHS Extends the Study

Vonderlehr and Wenger performed twenty spinal taps a day. When the spinal taps were completed in May 1933, the Tuskegee study was officially over, except for compiling the data that had been collected.

After assessing the information he had gathered, Vonderlehr wrote an article about the study. Printed in the September 1936 issue of *Venereal Disease Information*, the article showed that 46.6 percent of the men with syphilis showed signs of cardiovascular disease and 26.1 percent had clinical evidence of neurosyphilis. When his results were compared with those from the Norway research project, Vonderlehr claimed that the relatively high percentage of cardiovascular damage indicated that syphilis caused more heart-related problems in blacks than in whites. The study had thus accomplished its goal, which was to determine whether syphilis affected blacks and whites differently.

The fate of the study, however, took a dramatic turn in June when Clark retired as director of the PHS's Division of Venereal Diseases and Vonderlehr succeeded him. Although Clark had authorized the study to run for only a short period, Vonderlehr believed that further research was needed. In fact, as early as April 8, 1933, Vonderlehr had written Clark to suggest that the study be extended:

> At the end of this project we shall have a considerable number of cases representing various complications of syphilis, who have received only mercury and may still be considered untreated in the modern sense of therapy. Should these cases be followed over a period from five to ten years many interesting facts can be learned regarding the course and complications of untreated syphilis. [It] seems a pity to me to lose such an unusual opportunity.[30]

Vonderlehr succeeded in persuading PHS officials to extend the Tuskegee study, and now he decided to add a new element to it—autopsies of the men when they died. In an autopsy, the body is cut open and the organs, such as the heart and brain, are removed and thoroughly examined and tested. The autopsies would allow researchers to gain much more detailed information about any physical damage the disease had caused. On July 18, Vonderlehr wrote to Wenger about his idea for the autopsies:

Long-Term Effects of Syphilis

When people first become infected with syphilis, they develop sores and rashes on their bodies. These outward signs of the disease usually disappear after a few weeks or months. The disease then goes through an inactive phase for several years during which it does not harm the person physically. From three to fifteen years after the initial infection, however, some people will enter the third stage of syphilis. This occurs because the syphilis bacteria have continued to reproduce, forming soft, tumorlike tissues called gummas in the person's bones, skin, nervous tissue, heart, and arteries. The gummas are very destructive and cause a wide variety of medical problems.

Syphilis causes two basic types of damage to the body. Cardiovascular syphilis attacks the heart and blood vessels, which weakens a person and can eventually lead to death. Neurosyphilis affects the brain, spinal cord, and spinal nerves, causing a wide variety of devastating symptoms. These include loss of muscular control, paralysis, stroke, mental illness, seizures, and hallucinations.

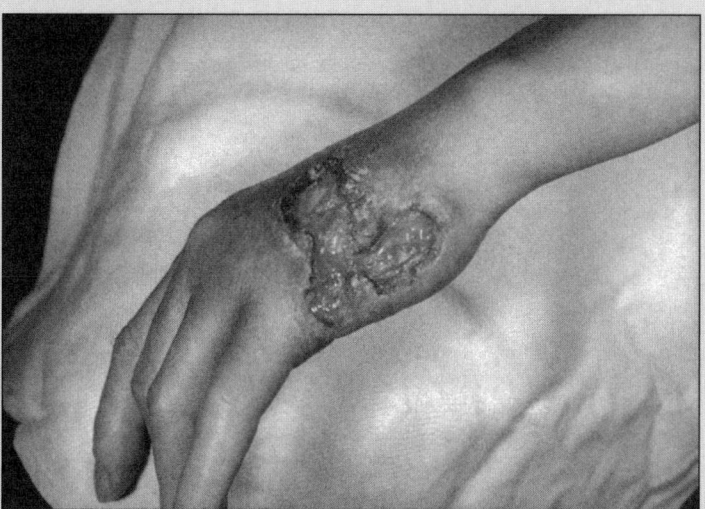

In advanced stages of syphilis, soft tumorlike tissues known as gummas begin to appear on the skin and other parts of the body.

Everyone is agreed that the proper procedure is the continuance of the observation of the Negro men used in the study with the idea of eventually bringing them to autopsy. I realize that this may be impracticable in connection with some of the younger cases [it would take many years for them to die], but those more advanced in age with serious complications of the vital organs should have to be followed for only a period of a few years.[31]

An Immoral Study

It was at this point that experts in medical ethics say the Tuskegee study became immoral. When Clark had originally proposed the study, it involved withholding treatment from the men for a few months, a short period that would not significantly harm them. But Vonderlehr now wanted to study men with a serious disease until they died, and without ever treating them for it. Syphilis can take decades to kill its victims, and during this period they can suffer serious health problems.

This callous disregard for the lives and health of the men over four decades would make the Tuskegee study one of the most unethical research projects in medical history. As Wenger noted in a July 21 letter to Vonderlehr in which he backed continuing the research, "As I see it, we have no further interest in these patients until they die."[32]

A New Direction

In his letter to Vonderlehr, Wenger made a series of suggestions about whom to contact in Alabama's government to win support for the prolonged study as well as how to handle the autopsies. Wenger also stressed the necessity of gaining the cooperation of local physicians to make sure they would not treat the study's participants for syphilis. PHS officials eventually did this by compiling a list of the names of the men in the study who had syphilis and giving it to all the local doctors.

With the backing of Surgeon General Cumming, Vonderlehr was able to convince local doctors and health officials to support the continuation of the study. He also won the cooperation of the Tuskegee Institute, whose medical facilities the PHS needed to continue examining the men.

Dr. John R. Heller directed the operations of the Tuskegee study. He dispensed aspirin and vitamins to dupe the subjects into thinking they were receiving treatment.

Vonderlehr appointed Dr. John R. Heller of the PHS to run the Tuskegee study's on-site medical operations. When Heller arrived in Tuskegee in November, some of the men who had been part of the original short-term study began coming to Andrew Hospital in hopes of receiving more free treatment for their "bad blood." Because the PHS wanted the men to cooperate with the study, Heller dispensed colored aspirin and other inexpensive medicine to the men so they would think they were being treated.

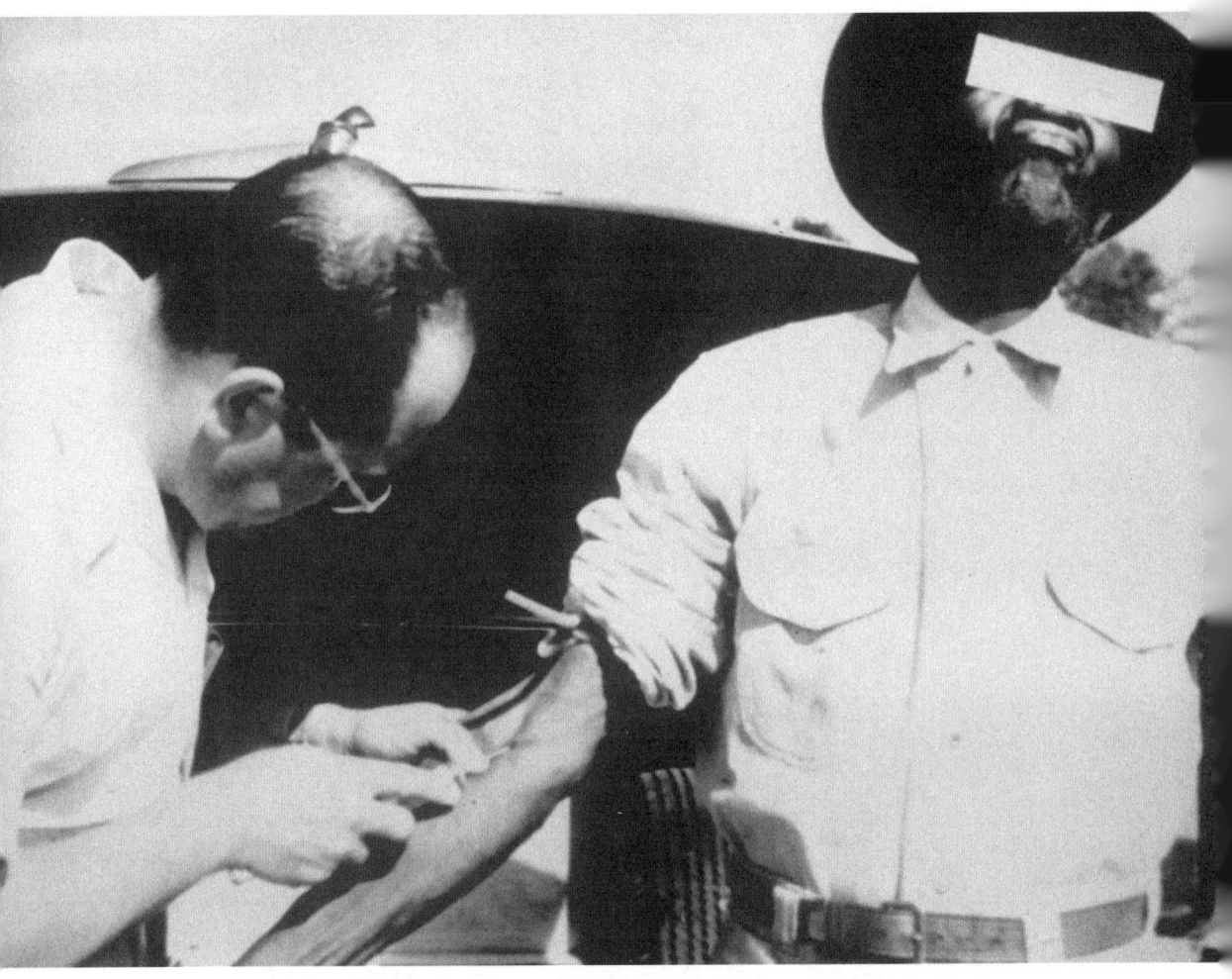

An unidentified Tuskegee study subject winces in pain during a test. Many of the study's participants sickened and died as their syphilis went untreated.

Heller also began performing new examinations of the men in the original study as well as on blacks whose tests in 1932 had shown they did not have syphilis. He wanted to select a control group of black males who did not have syphilis so that their rates of death and illness could be compared with those of the men who had the disease.

In selecting men for both groups for the new, extended phase of the Tuskegee study, the PHS chose men middle-aged and older—56 percent of the men were at least forty years of age, with about 5 percent at least seventy—because the disease could be expected to be more advanced in them. Members of the control group had to be similar in age so that the health comparisons between the two groups would be meaningful. In the end, 399 men afflicted with syphilis were chosen. An additional 201 men who did not have the disease were placed in the control group, a group that was used as a standard for comparisons in medical experiments.

Deceit for Four Decades

The Tuskegee study now took on a life of its own. It was never supposed to have lasted more than a few months, but once it began, it continued for four decades. For that entire time, doctors lied to the men about their medical condition. Dr. Sidney Olansky, who directed the study in the 1950s, recalled years later that it had been easy to mislead the men about the truth of the study because of their ignorance of medical matters. "The fact that they were illiterate was helpful, too," he added, "because they couldn't read the newspapers. If they were not [illiterate], as things moved on they might have been reading newspapers and seen what was going on."[33]

The ability of the doctors to continue to deceive the men allowed them to extend the original study far beyond its original completion date. This had dire consequences for the men involved, many of whom sickened and died as the syphilis that was eating away at their bodies went untreated.

Chapter Three

The Tuskegee Study Continues for Decades

When, in October 1932, the U.S. Public Health Service began offering free blood tests in Macon County, Alabama, as part of its search for suitable subjects for the Tuskegee Study of Untreated Syphilis in the Negro Male, there was no lack of volunteers. So many people responded to the offer to be tested for "bad blood" that, according to Eunice Rivers, the nurse who helped administer the tests, the PHS teams were "overflooded with people coming in to get their blood drawn." She also stated that "[most] had never been to a doctor—never seen one."[34]

Out of the black men who came that fall to have their blood drawn and tested, 399 with syphilis and 201 as a control group were chosen to receive continued care for a medical condition doctors identified to them only as "bad blood." Because the subjects in the study knew little about medical matters, it was easy for the PHS to make them believe they needed continuing care for the vaguely defined illness. The men were also grateful because they believed they were receiving medical care that their friends and neighbors could not afford.

It was their faith in doctors, ignorance of medical matters, and desire to continue the treatment for their vaguely identified condition that kept the men in the study coming back year after year for follow-up testing. For four decades, they never realized they were actually subjects in a long-term study of how syphilis affected people when it was left untreated.

How the Study Operated

Once the six hundred men had been selected in early 1934, the study settled into a simple routine. Each year the PHS gave the men in the study new blood tests and physical examinations as well as supplies of "medicine" for their "bad blood." This medicine consisted of pink-colored aspirin, iron tonic (which was referred to as "spring tonic"), and vitamins, none of which would have any effect on syphilis.

Nurse Eunice Rivers interacts with a Tuskegee test subject at work in a cotton field. It was Rivers's job to help set participants' minds at ease.

Starting in 1938 and approximately every four years after that, the men were also given more complete physicals in order to monitor more closely how the disease was affecting them. Because almost all of the men worked in agriculture, the examinations were done in late January or early February, a slack period between the busy fall harvest and spring planting seasons.

In 1973, after the study's existence became known, Charles Pollard, one of the men in the study, explained how the annual examinations were conducted: "They would take out blood [to

Racial Deceit

■

In *Bad Blood: The Tuskegee Syphilis Experiment*, author James H. Jones explains that even when the Tuskegee study began, the doctors who conducted it understood that it had important racial implications because all of the test subjects were black. Jones said that because of this, the doctors used different terms when describing the study to whites and blacks:

> The PHS's nomenclature in presenting the experiment broke on racial lines. A curious protocol was employed, one that revealed a great deal about Dr. Vonderlehr's sense of the racial etiquette that would have to be followed in order to ensure the cooperation of the Tuskegee Institute's black leaders. When health officers corresponded among themselves or with other white physicians, they invariably described the experiment as a study of the effects of syphilis on the "Negro male." But when they discussed the experiment with Dr. Moton and [Tuskegee Institute doctor. Eugene H.] Dibble [who were black], they were careful to refer to it as a study of the effects of syphilis on the "human economy." The change in wording was significant, for it altered the appearance of the study from an investigation of race and disease to one of people and disease. No one was fooled by the word game [about the study's racial implications].

test it]. They would just give us the pills and sometimes they would give us a little tablet to put under our tongue for sore throats. They would give us the green medicine for a tonic to take after meals."[35]

Herman Shaw, another subject in the study, said doctors at the annual exams never told the men if the "bad blood" condition they supposedly had was getting better or worse. "I just got a slap on the back and they said you are good [to live for another] 100 years. That is all I ever had,"[36] said Shaw. The joking comment that Shaw was healthy enough to live for a century was typical of the lack of information the men received on their condition. Even the men with syphilis who were beginning to develop serious health problems were never told any details about their medical condition.

Both the annual checkups and the more extensive four-year examinations were performed at John A. Andrew Memorial Hospital at the Tuskegee Institute, the black college located in Tuskegee, Alabama, where the earlier spinal taps and other tests had been done. The PHS did not keep a doctor in Tuskegee year-round. Instead, it hired Rivers in 1932 to serve as the government's primary contact with the men and their families.

"A Picnic Atmosphere"

The yearly examinations were the accustomed contact between the men in the study and the PHS officials. According to Dr. Sidney Olansky, who was in charge of the program from 1950 to 1955, the men looked forward to the annual opportunity to socialize with each other and with medical personnel like Rivers, the nurse whom they came to know well through the years. Said Olansky: "It was a picnic atmosphere. We did the bloods [blood tests], then we'd eat sandwiches, and they'd all sit around and sing. We had fun."[37]

Because many of the men lived a dozen or more miles from the hospital and had no way to get there, Rivers would drive around Macon County to pick them up two at a time for the examinations. While one man was being examined, she and the other man would tour the Tuskegee Institute or go into town. Most of the men rarely traveled more than a few miles from their homes, so they enjoyed these excursions. Rivers would then take the men home and pick up two more subjects for examinations. She usually made two round trips each day to bring men to the hospital. Rivers said the men always had a good time: "In the early days, the people enjoyed the trip."[38]

Keeping the Men Involved

The doctors who ran the study wanted all the men to stay involved in the research until they died in order to have as much data as possible on the long-term effects of syphilis. The free physical examinations and medicine were important in keeping the men involved in the project. However, PHS doctors also used a variety of other incentives to make sure the men would continue to participate in the study.

One small reward was to serve the men free meals when they came to the hospital. Although the meal was only a lunch in the hospital cafeteria, it was a treat for poor men who often had little variety in their diet, and it also saved them a little money.

The PHS also promised two other financial incentives. On the study's twenty-fifth anniversary, the agency would give each man a certificate and $25, one dollar for each year they had been receiving care. The most important inducement to their continued participation in the study, however, was the $50 each man's family was to be given toward burial expenses when he died. This money came from a grant from the Milbank Memorial Fund, a charity that supported medical research. The payment was enough in the early years to pay for a funeral. Dr. Olansky claimed that the payment helped win the cooperation of almost every family because "burial is very important to those people."[39]

The doctors who ran the Tuskegee study believed that they needed to offer such incentives to the men and their families to make sure they would stay in contact with the PHS and continue coming back for examinations year after year. Their reasoning about such incentives was explained in a 1953 report on the Tuskegee study written by doctors involved in it:

Because of the low educational status of the majority of the patients, it was impossible to appeal to them from a purely scientific approach. Therefore, various methods were used to maintain and stimulate their interest. Free medicines,

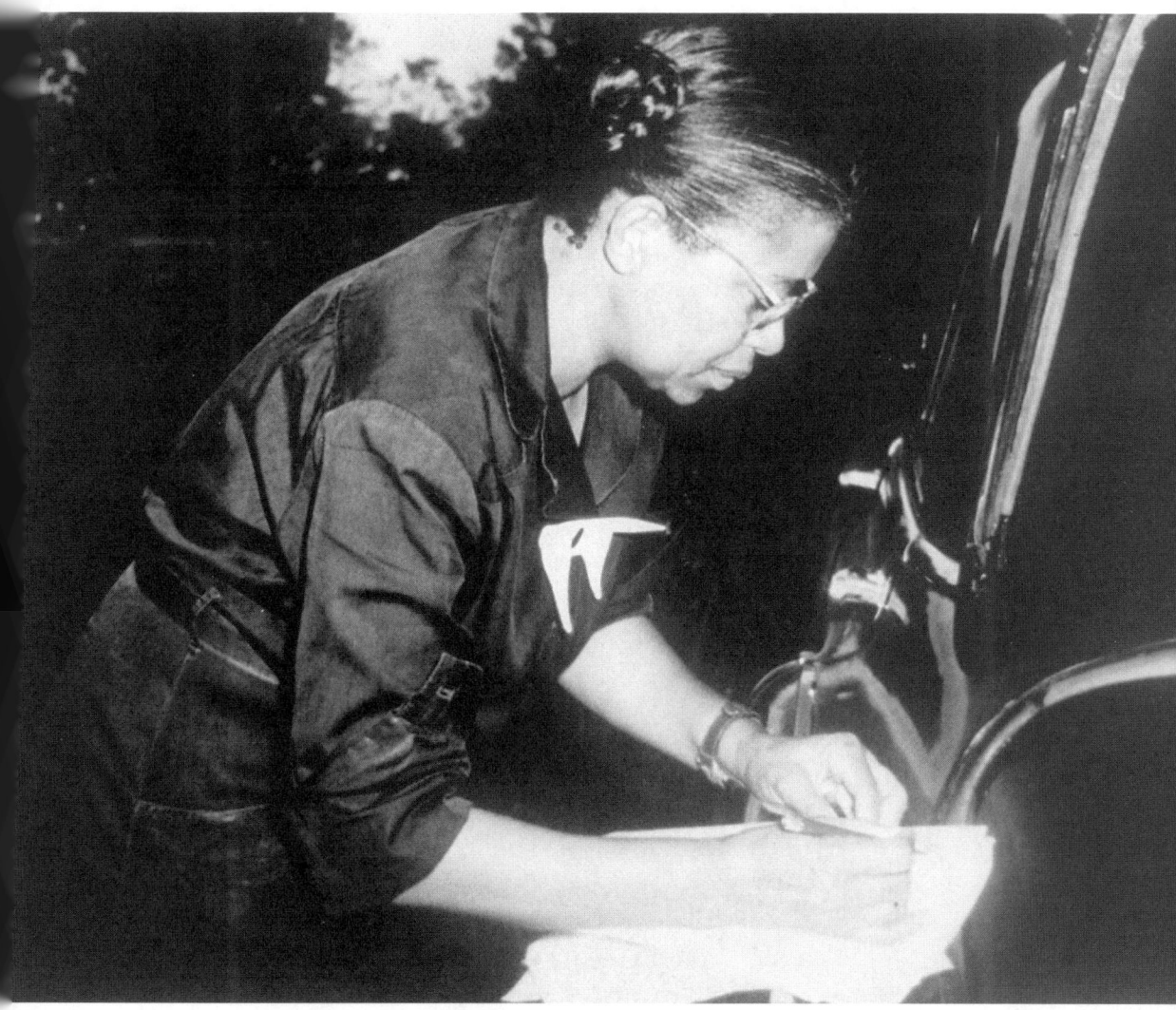

In 1932 the Public Health Service hired nurse Rivers to serve as the primary liaison between the government and the test subjects.

burial assistance or insurance, free hot meals on the days of examination, transportation to and from the hospital, and an opportunity to stop in town on the return trip to shop or visit with their friends on the streets all helped.[40]

A free lunch and even small sums of money were important at the time to people who could not afford medical care and who rarely traveled more than a few miles from their homes. Rivers explains that the small favors made the men feel special because other blacks did not get them:

> When these men were brought in [for examinations], it was just like you would be thinking about going to New York with them, to get a chance to come to Tuskegee and spend the day. It meant everything in the world to the patient to get a physical exam [because] here was a group of men out of a community where [black] folks had never seen any

A doctor and his assistants take X-rays of an unidentified study subject at Tuskegee's John A. Andrew Memorial Hospital.

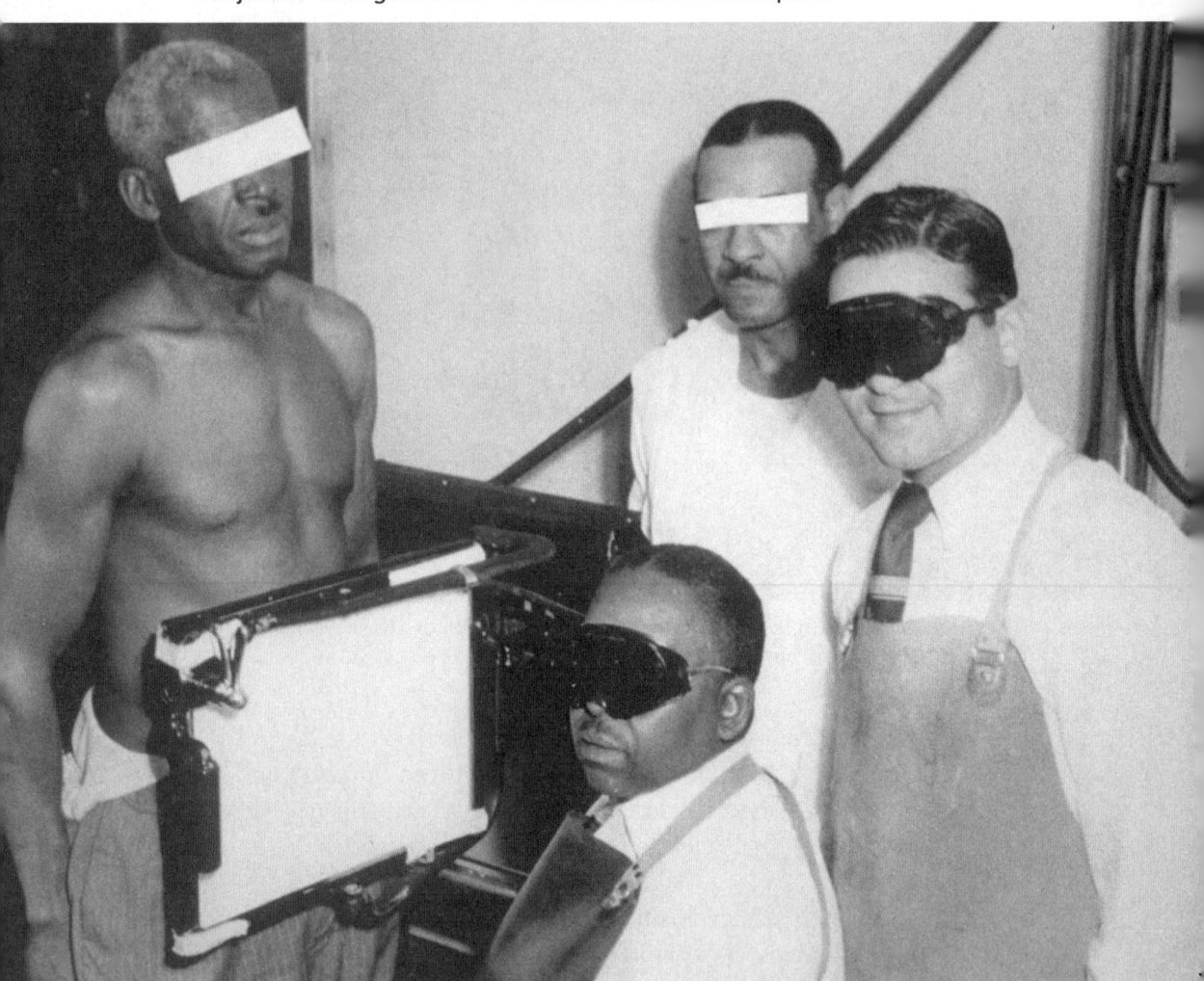

doctors and [they felt like] they were really somebody to have somebody give that kind of attention to them.[41]

Misrepresenting Autopsies

Autopsies were a key part of the study because they provided a new level of scientific data on how untreated syphilis affected the men physically over the years. In 1932 Wenger warned Vonderlehr that convincing families to allow the autopsies might be difficult because the procedure involves cutting up a body and removing organs. Wenger believed that many families would refuse to allow this medical procedure to be done to their loved ones because it would disfigure their bodies.

In language that clearly shows the racist attitudes the doctors often displayed toward the men, Wenger wrote to Vonderlehr on July 21, "If the colored population becomes aware that accepting free hospital care means a post-mortem [autopsy], every darky [a racist term for a black person] will leave Macon County."[42] Because Vonderlehr understood such fears, he once again decided to mislead the men and their families by not making it clear from the beginning that autopsies would be required when the men died. "Naturally, it is not my intention to let it be generally known that the main object of the present activities is the bringing of the men to [autopsy],"[43] he wrote in response to Wenger's letter.

The $50 burial payment was a powerful incentive in persuading the families to allow the autopsies. The 1953 report stated that in the first twenty years of the study, the family of only one of the 146 men who died refused permission for an autopsy. Because Rivers was always the person who went to the families to secure permission for an autopsy when someone died, the men in the study began to joke among themselves that they belonged to "Miss Rivers' Lodge." (A lodge is a social organization that among its benefits often provides its members with money for funeral expenses.) The report also boasted that by the early 1950s, the participants themselves were helping to make sure autopsies were done when other men died: "Now, after many years, all of the patients are aware of the autopsies. When a member of 'Miss Rivers' Lodge' passes, his surviving colleagues often will remind the family that the doctor wants 'to look at his heart.' Autopsies today are a routine."[44]

Nurse Rivers

The nickname "Miss Rivers' Lodge" was symbolic of the affectionate relationship the nurse established with the men in the study. The many doctors who were involved in the study through the years all praised Rivers for her ability to gain the cooperation of the men and their families in the various facets of the research project, including the autopsies. The 1953 published report on the study offered the following explanation for the nurse's success in working with the men:

> One cannot work with a group of people over a long period of time without becoming attached to them. This has been the experience of the nurse. She has had an opportunity to know them personally. She has come to understand some of their problems. The ties are stronger than simply those of patient and nurse. There is a feeling of complete confidence in what the nurse advises.[45]

Rivers was able to inspire confidence in the men she worked with because she had lived among them for many years and was from a similar background: She was black and had grown up on a farm in rural Georgia. The men in the study liked and trusted her. "She was always my favorite,"[46] claimed Herman Shaw, one of the men in the study who had syphilis.

Rivers had graduated from the Tuskegee Institute School of Nursing in 1922 and had worked for the Alabama State Department of Health for several years before returning to Tuskegee's hospital as head night nurse. She was one of only four black nurses in Alabama. Selected to help with the Rosenwald Fund syphilis demonstration project in 1930, Rivers continued to work with the Tuskegee study's participants until it ended.

Through all the long years of the study, the hardest part of the job for Rivers was helping perform the autopsies. The procedure upset her greatly the first few times she assisted with it. "I hadn't had that experience. It wasn't an easy thing to see them do those autopsies,"[47] she later admitted.

She found it much easier to visit the homes of the men who had died to make sure their families would allow the autopsy. She would try to ease the family's fears about what would happen to

Nurse Rivers and the Autopsies

In an autopsy, doctors cut open a body to examine organs such as the heart, liver, and brain to assess physical damage from disease. In a 1977 interview taken from Reverby's *Tuskegee's Truths*, nurse Eunice Rivers explained that the families of test subjects in the Tuskegee study were worried that the autopsies would ruin the way their loved ones looked in death. She said that because the procedure seemed so strange to the family members, they feared other people would learn that an autopsy had been performed. For this reason, they did not want the body to show any signs of the autopsy at the funeral:

> I had to explain to [the families] what the procedures were. I had to guarantee them that they would not mar the body. They didn't want the public to know that we had cut the body, the family didn't. I had to make [the doctor] promise that he would not mar the body where it would be exposed [at a funeral]. And he wouldn't. He was always very, very careful about it. If we went into the [head], we always did, you know, the incision in the back. We made *sure* that the face was not marred. We never marred any and . . . I just felt that was my responsibility. I would not want somebody to do that [physical damage] to a member of my family. And this was the way I felt about them.

the body during the autopsy by claiming it was like an "operation," a word that made it sound like a benefit. Rivers firmly believed she was helping the families by persuading them to go ahead with the autopsies because the stipend meant a lot to poor people. "In those early days fifty dollars was a whole heap of money for a funeral,"[48] she said.

Rivers would sit for hours with the families of the men who died, trying to console them. "I was expected to be there. They were part of my family,"[49] she said in a 1977 interview. During the many years of the study, Rivers came to care about the men and their families and enjoyed the time she spent with them. Said

Rivers: "Oh, we had a good time. We had a good time. Really and truly, when we were working with those people that was the joy of my life."[50]

A Case of Betrayal?

For many historians, Rivers is the most intriguing and controversial personality in the Tuskegee study. Some have condemned the nurse for participating in a research project that endangered the lives of people, especially because they were of her own race. Indeed, much of the criticism of her part in the study is due to the fact that she helped white doctors abuse the rights of black men by tricking them into participating in the study.

Nurse Rivers poses with Public Health Service officials. Some critics have blasted her as a traitor to her race, while others have defended her role in the study.

Many historians, however, temper any criticism of Rivers by noting that as a black woman in the racist South, she had no power to stop what was happening. In his book about the Tuskegee study, Fred R. Gray exonerates her by writing: "Nurse Rivers was a lone African American female working on a health program financed by the federal government. She was working directly with white doctors [and] neither the racial climate [of the time] nor society's attitudes toward government encouraged her questioning the activities of white government officials."[51]

"Just Talk to Them Like They're People"

Defenders of Nurse Rivers also point out that even though she helped with the study, she was also fiercely protective of the men involved and demanded that doctors treat them with respect. The white doctors, however, sometimes used racist language toward the men and even hurt them physically by the careless way they examined them. One man once told Rivers that a doctor hurt him when he took a blood sample: "He lay my arm down like he guttin' a hog. I told him he hurt me. He told me 'I'm the doctor.' I told him all right but this my arm."[52]

When that man or others complained to Rivers about how doctors treated them, she would tell the physicians to change their ways. Rivers said to one doctor who had used racist language toward a test subject: "You don't have to pet them; you don't have to beg them. Just talk to them man to man. Just talk to them; they understand. You don't have to get on your knees to them, but just be polite to them. Just talk to them like they're people."[53] After Rivers delivered that lecture, the doctor apologized to the man he had offended. The fact that Rivers championed the men in such situations deepened the close ties she had with them and made them trust her even more.

Such behavior also showed how much Rivers cared for the men. And although Rivers knew the true nature of the Tuskegee study and the physical effects the syphilis would inflict on the men when left untreated, she did not believe she was doing anything wrong. In fact, Rivers believed the study actually helped the men in a variety of small ways. For example, she once explained that doctors sometimes treated the men for an unrelated illness, such as a cold, when they came in for their examinations. Rivers once said of her work in the study: "I don't have any regrets. You can't regret doing what you did when you knew you were doing right. I feel I did good in working with the people. I know I didn't mislead anyone."[54]

Rivers, however, was not the only black person who helped conduct or who knew about the controversial study involving African Americans. Tuskegee Institute officials initially approved the study, and several black doctors helped perform medical examinations of the men involved. However, like the test subjects themselves, most of the other blacks did not know the true nature of the study. Dr. Joshua Williams, an intern at John A. Andrew Memorial Hospital in 1932, said, "We thought it [the study] was merely a service group organized to help the people in the area. We didn't know it was a research project at all at the time."[55] And on November 27, 1941, Dr. Murray Smith, the Macon County health officer, wrote a letter to Vonderlehr complaining about Tuskegee officials: "[They] are not the same ones that you and I had such fine cooperation with a few years ago. They know nothing about the study."[56] Thus as time went by, it seems that fewer and fewer people outside the PHS knew the truth about the study.

One black physician who did know, however, was Dr. Paul B. Cornely. In an interview in 1989, Cornely said that he was aware of the study from the beginning and discussed it with medical students he taught at Howard University, a historically black institution in Washington, D.C. Saying that he had "guilt feelings," Cornely also admitted that he did nothing to stop the study despite knowing that it was ignoring the serious health problems the men with syphilis had. Said Cornely, "I was there and I didn't say a word. I saw it [the study] as an academician. It shows you how we looked at human beings, especially blacks who were expendable."[57]

Test Subjects, Not Human Beings

Even more extreme than Cornely's attitude was that of the government officials who ran the study. Many of the white doctors involved in the study considered the black participants ignorant and inferior. In some cases the physicians even made light of the

Blacks Helped Conduct the Study

African American doctors and medical personnel like Eunice Rivers have been criticized for the roles they played in the Tuskegee study. In February 2001 during Black History Month, the *Jacksonville Free Press* commented on that in a story it ran on the study:

It takes little imagination to ascribe racist attitudes to the white government officials who ran the experiment, but what can one make of the numerous African Americans who collaborated with them? The experiment's name comes from the Tuskegee Institute, the black university founded by Booker T. Washington. Its affiliated hospital lent the PHS its medical facilities for the study, and other predominantly black institutions as well as local black doctors also participated. A black nurse, Eunice Rivers, was a central figure in the experiment for most of its forty years. The promise of recognition by a prestigious government agency may have obscured the troubling aspects of the study for some. A Tuskegee doctor, for example, praised "the educational advantages offered our interns and nurses as well as the added standing it will give the hospital." Nurse Rivers explained her role as one of passive obedience: "We [as nurses] were taught that we never diagnosed, we never prescribed; we followed the doctor's instructions!" It is clear that the men in the experiment trusted her and that she sincerely cared about their well-being, but her unquestioning submission to authority eclipsed her moral judgment.

pain that procedures like spinal taps caused the men. In a 1933 letter to Vonderlehr, Dr. Murray Smith spoke in gleeful tones of the reaction some of the men displayed when they saw him driving through Macon County: "Wish you could see some of the Old S.P. [spinal puncture] brethren scram to the woods when they see me, as I go over the county now."[58]

The Tuskegee Institute, a college for blacks in Tuskegee, Alabama, gave its name to the infamous syphilis study that took place there.

A lack of a sense that they were studying human beings is also evident in some researchers' reports about the ongoing study. In these documents they expressed no concern that the untreated men were growing sick and dying from a disease they did not even know they had. In 1946 the second published report on the Tuskegee study explained that the disease had shortened the lives of the men with syphilis. The report noted that after the study's first twelve years the death rate of the men in the control group who did not have syphilis was 14 percent, compared to 25 percent for those who had syphilis. The article ended by saying, "In conclusion, it can be said that the life expectancy of a negro man between the ages of 25 and 50 who is infected with syphilis and receives no treatment for the infection is on the average reduced by about 20 percent."[59] The article made no apologies for the fact that the study, by denying the men treatment for the disease, was itself responsible for the higher death rate.

Predictions About the Study

It was this apparent lack of remorse that angered millions of people in 1972 when details of the project were finally made public. At that point, two predictions made forty years earlier by two doctors involved in the study came true.

In 1932 Dr. Taliaferro Clark and Dr. Oliver Wenger had made predictions about the study's outcome. Clark believed that the study would become a landmark in syphilis research; in a letter to a colleague he boasted, "I am confident the results of this study, if anywhere near our expectations, will attract worldwide attention." Wenger was more wary. In a letter to a friend, he expressed the fear that the study could have negative consequences: "It will either cover us with mud or glory when completed."[60]

Four decades later, the predictions of both men came true. When the Tuskegee study was revealed to the public in 1972, it did attract the world's attention. And because of the way the subjects had been treated, everyone who had ever been connected with it became covered with "mud" in the form of negative publicity.

Chapter Four

Questions and Problems Arise

Early in the Tuskegee Study of Untreated Syphilis in the Negro Male, Dr. Raymond Vonderlehr shared with several nationally respected medical experts some of the initial data that had been gathered. One of them was Dr. H.M. Marvin, president of the American Heart Association (AHA). Vonderlehr sent Marvin the results because the tests on the men with syphilis had shown they suffered from high levels of cardiovascular syphilis and low levels of neurosyphilis. According to Vonderlehr, this proved that the disease affected blacks differently than it did whites, who scientists at the time believed would experience more neurosyphilis damage than blacks.

But when Marvin responded with a letter on August 2, 1933, he did not share Vonderlehr's excitement over the research results. Instead, the AHA president criticized the study's scientific validity. Marvin thought that the findings were probably inaccurate. He argued that they were based on limited medical examinations that failed to thoroughly test the condition of the patients. Marvin also criticized Vonderlehr's interpretation of the data as faulty and said Vonderlehr had relied too heavily on X-rays to make his diagnoses. In fact, Marvin wrote, "I will say quite frankly that conclusions based upon the observations indicated in your letter would be regarded by me as of very little if any value [because the tests and procedures] are all open to serious criticism."[61]

In October 1933 an AHA committee raised similar concerns about the study's findings. Vonderlehr, however, ignored these criticisms of the validity of the research. In fact, most of the people who worked on the study in its four decades would repeatedly ignore criticism and negative comments about the study, which ranged from how it was conducted to the medical ethics involved in using human beings in a long-range medical research project. In *Bad Blood: The Tuskegee Syphilis Experiment*, author James H. Jones notes that the Public Health Service believed that the study was so important that it had to continue no matter what problems, criticism, or opposition it encountered:

A medical technician labels a vial of blood for the Tuskegee study. Despite early criticism of the scientific validity of the study, doctors continued with the long-term project.

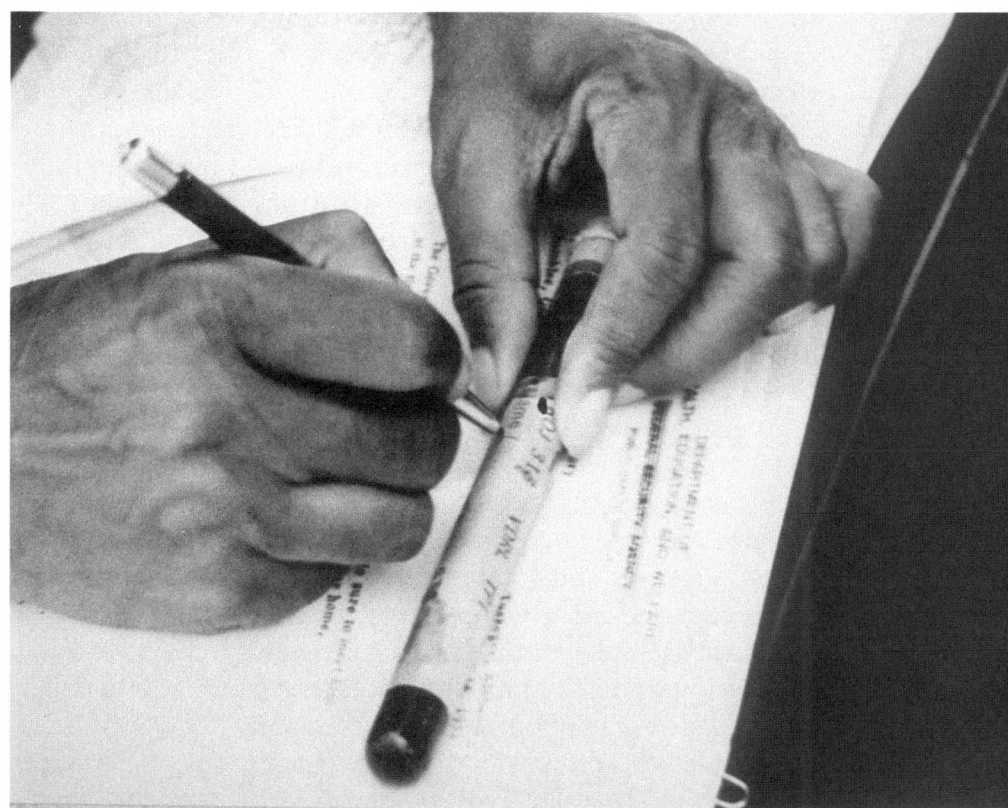

On the few occasions when [the study was challenged] directly, a defender [from the PHS] invariably pointed out how long it had been going on, how much work the PHS had invested, and how science would benefit if the study continued. The results were to increase its [official] momentum, making it largely self-perpetuating.[62]

Flaws in the Study

Most PHS officials were so committed to continuing the Tuskegee study that they even ignored major flaws in the design of the research project itself. The first serious challenge to the study's design was raised not by an outsider but by a PHS doctor. In the fall of 1938 Vonderlehr assigned Dr. Austin V. Deibert to go to Tuskegee and give the men in the study complete physical examinations. The physicals were the first of several full-scale examinations the men would receive throughout the course of the study to assess the toll that the untreated syphilis was taking on their health. Shortly after Deibert began his work, he was surprised to learn from the men's medical histories that many of them had received at least some treatment for syphilis.

On November 28, 1938, Deibert wrote to Vonderlehr that the treatment the men had already received would make the study's results meaningless: "I firmly believe that we cannot obtain a true reflection of the course of untreated syphilis in view of 40 percent of the cases having had some treatment."[63] Deibert was referring to the medical care many of the men had been given during the 1930 Rosenwald Fund syphilis control project as well as in the first few months of the original Tuskegee study.

Vonderlehr already knew that a significant number of the men in the study had received some treatment with mercury ointment and injections of neoarsphenamine. But he had rationalized that the men had not received *enough* treatment to affect the outcome of the long-term study of untreated syphilis. However, historians believe that including these men in the study was a major flaw that invalidated the results from the beginning. As scholar Susan M. Reverby wrote, "Ultimately, the Tuskegee Study was of undertreated rather than of purely untreated syphilis."[64]

In order to correct this flaw and ensure that the research results would be valid, Deibert wanted to replace more than a

In 1938 PHS official Dr. Austin V. Deibert questioned the results of the study after he discovered that many of the subjects had previously received some form of syphilis treatment.

hundred of the men in the study who had received treatment. However, due to a shortage of funds he was able to remove only fourteen of them. The new subjects chosen to take their place had been examined originally for the study but had not been chosen to be included at the time. As Deibert continued to examine the men in the study, he made another discovery: A dozen men in the control group had contracted syphilis. Instead of dropping these men from the study, Deibert and Vonderlehr decided to simply move them to the group that had syphilis. Moving participants from the control group to the group with syphilis was another flaw in the study because it affected its long-term statistical results.

After those small changes were made, the study's rosters did not change again for its duration. However, record keeping was haphazard, with the result that for many years there were uncertainties as to how many men were actually being studied. Because

British researcher Alexander Fleming discovered penicillin in 1928. Although penicillin was an effective syphilis treatment, Tuskegee doctors did not administer it to participants.

of this uncertainty, historians writing about the Tuskegee study generally use the original figures for the number of men involved in the study: 399 men with syphilis and 201 in the control group, for a total of 600.

A New Cure, a Sinister Twist

What is certain is that when the Tuskegee study began, there was no sure cure for syphilis. However, while the study was going on, a new drug called penicillin emerged that would one day prove totally effective in curing the deadly disease. Penicillin would create further controversy about the study because PHS doctors refused to treat study participants with it even after it was proven effective against syphilis.

Penicillin had been discovered in 1928 by British scientist Alexander Fleming. Hailed as a wonder drug because it could kill bacteria, it was widely used by the U.S. military in World War II to combat a variety of infections that resulted from battle wounds. In the late 1940s penicillin became readily available to the general public and began to be used to treat many diseases, including syphilis.

Until penicillin was introduced as the standard cure for syphilis, doctors continued to rely on mercury ointment and arsenic-based drugs to fight the disease. Those treatments were not very effective, and in 1940 the death rate for syphilis was 10.7 people per 100,000 population. But by 1950, when penicillin had become the standard treatment for syphilis, that death rate had been cut by more than half to 5 per 100,000.

Most historians believe that the Tuskegee study entered a new, more sinister stage once penicillin was found to cure syphilis. It would have been easy to give the men penicillin shots, which could have prevented or even reversed some of the disastrous health effects of the disease. Historians note that the syphilis study in Norway in the late nineteenth century was stopped in 1910 after the discovery of arsphenamine, which at the time was considered a new, reliable cure for the disease. Even though that drug failed to fulfill its promise, researchers in Norway had believed it was no longer right to study men who had syphilis without providing them with what was at least a somewhat effective treatment.

"The Longer the Study, the Better"

PHS officials, however, never considered giving the men in the Tuskegee study penicillin when it became available. Dr. John R. Heller, who oversaw the study from 1942 until 1948, explained the doctors' interest in continuing to study the men without treating them: "The longer the study, the better the ultimate information we would derive."[65] Heller asserted that the data being collected was more important than the men themselves. He once explained his view of the participants, saying: "The men's status [as ill people] did not warrant ethical debate. They were subjects, not patients; clinical [research] material, not sick people."[66]

Not only was withholding penicillin from the men with syphilis unethical, it was actually illegal. In fact, the study itself had been in violation of Alabama state law since 1933, when PHS doctors had decided to continue the research until the men died. A 1927 law required county health officials to report and promptly treat anyone known to have syphilis. And in 1942 that regulation was strengthened by the Henderson Act, a strict public health law that required treatment of a number of diseases, including syphilis.

State and local officials, however, had always known that the study violated the law. When PHS officials explained the new direction the study was taking in 1933, state and local health officials gave their permission to study the men with syphilis without treating them. Alabama officials were persuaded by the PHS doctors' argument that the information they were gathering was valuable.

Preventing Treatment

Not only did the PHS fail to provide treatment for the infected men, but it went to great lengths to keep them from getting medical attention, especially treatment with penicillin, which researchers feared could contaminate the study's findings. At times during the four decades of the study, however, preventing the men in the study from receiving care for syphilis was a difficult task.

When the Tuskegee study first began, PHS doctors met with local physicians to explain the research. PHS doctors gave the local doctors a roster of the men in the study and asked the physicians not to treat the men for syphilis, even if they were treating

The Availability of Antibiotics

Although the Tuskegee study was supposed to track untreated syphilis, many of the men did receive varying amounts of care for the disease. The treatments even included penicillin, which when introduced in the 1940s became the first truly effective way to cure syphilis. In a 1978 article for the *Hastings Center Report*, Allan M. Brandt discussed this problem:

> In spite of efforts [by government doctors], by the early 1950s many of the men had secured some treatment on their own. By 1952, almost 30 percent of the test subjects had received some penicillin, although only 7.5 percent had received what could be considered adequate doses [to cure syphilis]. [Dr. Raymond] Vonderlehr wrote to one of the participating physicians, "I hope that the availability of antibiotics has not interfered too much with this project." A report published in 1955 [by the doctors involved] considered whether the treatment that some of the men had obtained had "defeated" the study. Any treatment which the men might have received, concluded the report, had been insufficient to compromise the experiment.

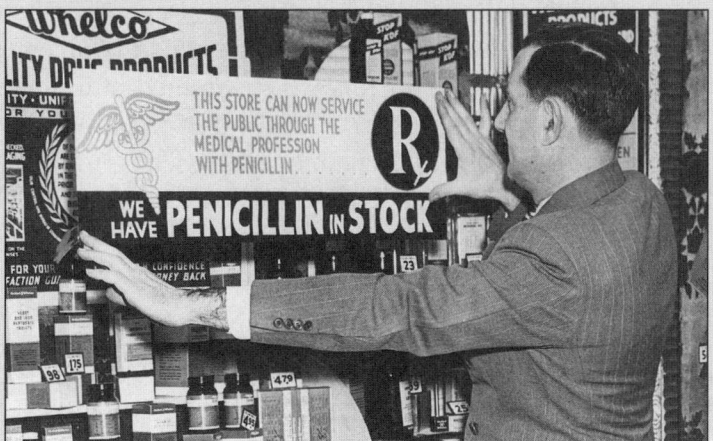

A pharmacist in 1945 posts a sign informing his customers of the availability of penicillin. Some of the Tuskegee subjects obtained penicillin through outside doctors.

them for other illnesses. Dr. Reginald D. James, who practiced in Macon County between 1939 and 1941, remembered how PHS officials worked with local doctors to enforce the treatment ban. "When we found [examined as a patient] one of the men from the Tuskegee Study [PHS officials] would say, 'He's under study and not to be treated,'"[67] James said.

A major challenge to preventing participants from receiving treatment occurred in 1942 when the United States began drafting soldiers for World War II. After some participants reported for physicals and were found to have syphilis, local officials were ready to refer them to local doctors for treatment. Vonderlehr, however, learned of the situation and acted quickly to prevent the men from receiving treatment. He asked Macon County draft officials to exclude blacks in the study from the requirement for such medical care. He succeeded in winning the draft board's cooperation. In a July 1942 letter to a local doctor he boasted, "So far, we are keeping the known positive patients from getting treatment."[68]

Because nurse Eunice Rivers was the one person connected with the study who was always in Tuskegee, she often had to prevent participants from being treated. And despite the friendships she had formed with many of the men, she was vigilant in this task. For example, in 1947 Herman Shaw, one of the men in the study who had syphilis, underwent a medical examination that was given by the Alabama state government as part of an effort to curb venereal disease. The doctors who examined him, unaware of his participation in the Tuskegee study, diagnosed him as suffering from syphilis. Shaw was taken by bus to a hospital in Birmingham for treatment. When Rivers heard this news, she informed doctors at the Birmingham hospital that Shaw was part of the Tuskegee study. They agreed not to treat him. Shaw remembered what happened next: "[The next morning] they gave me breakfast and put me on the bus and sent me back to Tuskegee. [The doctors told me,] 'You ain't supposed to be there—you're a Macon County patient.'"[69]

The Shaw incident today is considered one of the study's defining moments: Shaw was denied treatment with penicillin, which could have drastically improved his health. Many historians believe that by withholding this cure for syphilis from the men in the Tuskegee study, the doctors involved had forever crossed the line between what was ethical and what was not.

Medical Ethics

After World War II, a profound change in the way people viewed medical experiments involving human beings made the study seem especially immoral. The United States and other countries that had defeated the Nazi regime in Germany held a series of trials in the German city of Nuremberg to prosecute German soldiers and civilians for crimes committed during the war. One major trial in 1947 concerned twenty-three doctors who had conducted medical experiments on unwilling subjects who were prisoners in concentration camps. In many of the experiments, men, women, and children were subjected to conditions that amounted to physical torture and even resulted in death, such as immersion in ice-cold water to test how long it would take people to die.

The outcome of these trials was the Nuremberg Code, a ten-point statement on medical ethics that outlines the rights of people involved in medical experiments. The code requires researchers who perform medical studies to gain the consent of such persons and to fully explain to them the nature of the study, including any health dangers to which they might be exposed.

The Nuremberg Code was adopted by countries around the world, including the United States, as a safeguard against future atrocities on unwilling test subjects. The rights detailed in the Nuremberg Code were strengthened and expanded by the World Medical Association's Declaration of Helsinki in 1964. The declaration stated: "It is the duty of the physician in medical research to protect the life, health, privacy, and dignity of the human subject." It also mandated that "The subjects must be volunteers and informed participants in the research project."[70]

"To Me There Was No Similarity"

The Nuremberg Code and the Declaration of Helsinki changed the way the world conducted medical experiments, but the Tuskegee study continued, despite being a violation of both of these internationally recognized documents. The black men in the study had willingly submitted to medical examinations and received medicine for many years because they thought they were being treated for "bad blood." But they had never given their consent to be involved in a long-term study of syphilis. They did not even know they had the disease and had never been advised of the medical risks of remaining untreated for syphilis.

Even though no such ethical codes regarding medical experiments had been in place when the study began, experts on medical ethics say the new standards should have been applied to it following World War II. PHS officials were aware of the new medical ethics concerning human experiments, but they never

The Nuremberg Code

The Nuremberg Code is a ten-point statement that outlines the human rights that doctors must observe during medical experiments. This excerpt from the code is from the University of Michigan Internet site:

> The voluntary consent of the human subject is absolutely essential. This means that the person involved should have legal capacity to give consent; should be so situated as to be able to exercise free power of choice, without the intervention of any element of force, fraud, deceit, duress, over-reaching, or other ulterior form of constraint or coercion; and should have sufficient knowledge and comprehension of the elements of the subject matter involved, as to enable him to make an understanding and enlightened decision. This latter element requires that, before the acceptance of an affirmative decision by the experimental subject, there should be made known to him the nature, duration, and purpose of the experiment; the method and means by which it is to be conducted; all inconveniences and hazards reasonably to be expected; and the effects upon his health or person, which may possibly come from his participation in the experiment.

believed they had any bearing on the Tuskegee study. A comment by Heller years after the study ended shows how PHS personnel rationalized to themselves that the Tuskegee study did not violate standards of medical ethics such as those mandated by the Nuremberg Code. Heller said, "I, like most everybody else, was horrified at the things that were done [by the Nazis such as] doing experiments while the patients were not only alive but doing such things as would cause their deaths. To me there was no similarity at all between them [the Nazi experiments and the Tuskegee study]."[71]

Dissenting Doctors

As the study continued, however, some doctors did begin to make that connection between the Tuskegee study and the Nuremberg Code and to question the study's morality. One of the first to do this was Dr. Count D. Gibson Jr., who in 1955 heard Dr. Sidney Olansky, a PHS doctor who had worked on the study, discuss it during a seminar at the Medical College of Virginia. Gibson recalled being appalled by slides of autopsies that showed the severe physical damage that syphilis had done to men in the study: "My jaw dropped. I ran up to him [Olansky] afterwards and asked whether the people were getting penicillin and whether they were being kept in ignorance [of their disease]. He couldn't talk; he had to catch a plane."[72]

Gibson wrote Olansky a letter in which he argued that the men should be made aware of the nature of the study and their illness and should be treated. In his response, Olansky insisted, "I honestly feel that we have done them no real harm and probably have helped them in many ways."[73]

A decade later, in 1965, Dr. Irwin J. Schatz sent a letter to the PHS in which he also criticized the ethics underlying the Tuskegee study. Schatz had become angry after reading a 1964 article on the study. He wrote:

I am utterly astounded by the fact that physicians allow patients with a potentially fatal disease to remain untreated when effective therapy is available. I assume you feel that the information which is extracted is worth their sacrifice. If this is the case, then I suggest that the United States Public

Health Service and those physicians associated with it need to reevaluate their moral judgments in this regard.[74]

Unlike Gibson, Schatz never got an answer to his indignant letter, which was simply filed away with other complaints. It was not until 1970 that one of the study's own doctors would raise

Defending the Tuskegee Study

One reason the Tuskegee study continued for four decades is that the doctors who ran it constantly defended it as important medical research. Their impassioned belief that what they were doing was important made them ignore the study's practical and ethical problems. Dr. Oliver C. Wenger, who was involved in the study when it first started, was one of its strongest supporters. His defense is found in Susan M. Reverby's *Tuskegee's Truths: Rethinking the Tuskegee Syphilis Study*:

This is the last chance in our country to make an investigation of this sort. You may say, if that's so isn't the point rather academic. I don't think so. It may be academic so far as the patient who is treated, but you [as doctors] know even better than I, that you are not yet finding and treating all of the cases. Once again let me emphasize the importance of this quiet undertaking [the study] and urge that steps be taken so that it [the opportunity to study untreated syphilis] doesn't slip through our fingers.

Oliver C. Wenger, involved with the Tuskegee study from the start, remained one of its most loyal defenders.

some of the same issues. On September 10 of that year, Dr. James B. Lucas of the Venereal Diseases Branch of the PHS suggested ending the study because it was inconsistent with PHS goals of treating sick people. Lucas also complained that the study was scientifically flawed and had generally been a waste of time: "Nothing learned [in the study] will prevent, find, or cure a single case of infectious syphilis or bring us closer to our basic mission of controlling venereal disease in the United States."[75]

His warning went unheeded. The Tuskegee study continued for two more years until it finally became known to the public.

A Strange Defense

Doctors involved in the Tuskegee study routinely ignored complaints about the project, such as those by Gibson, Schatz, and Lucas. When the PHS doctors were forced to address such challenges, they invented a wide variety of arguments to justify the work they were doing because they believed it was too important to quit.

One of the most heartless defenses was put forth on September 18, 1950, by Dr. Wenger. Nearly two decades after he first became involved in the study, Wenger admitted to other doctors in a seminar that many of the men in the study had suffered harm by not being treated for syphilis. Astonishingly, however, Wenger went on to use their suffering as a further justification to continue the study: "We know now, where we could only surmise before, that we have contributed to their ailments and shortened their lives. I think the least we can say is that we have a high moral obligation to those that have died to make this the best study possible."[76]

Wenger's comments show that people involved with the Tuskegee study saw the research they were doing as more important than the lives of the men they were studying. It was that disregard for the men suffering from syphilis, as well as their families, that would inflame the world in 1972 when the study was finally made public.

Chapter Five

The Tuskegee Study: A National Scandal

As the years passed, many of the men in the Tuskegee Study of Untreated Syphilis in the Negro Male became sicker and sicker from the disease. They suffered from heart disease; problems with their eyesight, including blindness; loss of muscular control; and a variety of psychological problems caused by lesions that formed on their brains. Many of the men died of syphilis.

Despite the study's serious ethical and legal violations, Public Health Service doctors never tried to keep the study secret. In fact, between 1936 and 1972, researchers and medical personnel involved with the study wrote thirteen scholarly articles about what they had learned. Because their findings were published in medical journals read by only a small number of people, however, the general public never discovered what was happening.

Those reports documented the men's health problems and showed that the deterioration of their health accelerated as the study went on. PHS officials continued the study because they believed it was more important to learn about the disease than to save the lives of the men involved in the research. Finally, however, a PHS employee became so upset at the injustice being done to the Alabama men that he did something about it. His name was Peter Buxton, and his single-handed efforts would eventually put an end to the Tuskegee study.

Peter Buxton

In December 1965 Buxton began working in San Francisco at a PHS clinic that treated people with sexually transmitted diseases. Buxton's job was to interview people who sought medical help at the clinic and investigate their cases to see if their sexual partners also needed care. Buxton learned of the Tuskegee study when he heard coworkers discussing it. Interested in finding out more, Buxton requested copies of past reports on the study from the U.S. Centers for Disease Control (CDC).

The articles detailed how the federal government had operated a study that allowed men with syphilis to go untreated for four decades. Buxton was shocked; he believed the government's failure

A Tuskegee study participant undergoes an electrocardiogram. Despite the ethical violations of the study, researchers firmly believed their work served the greater scientific good.

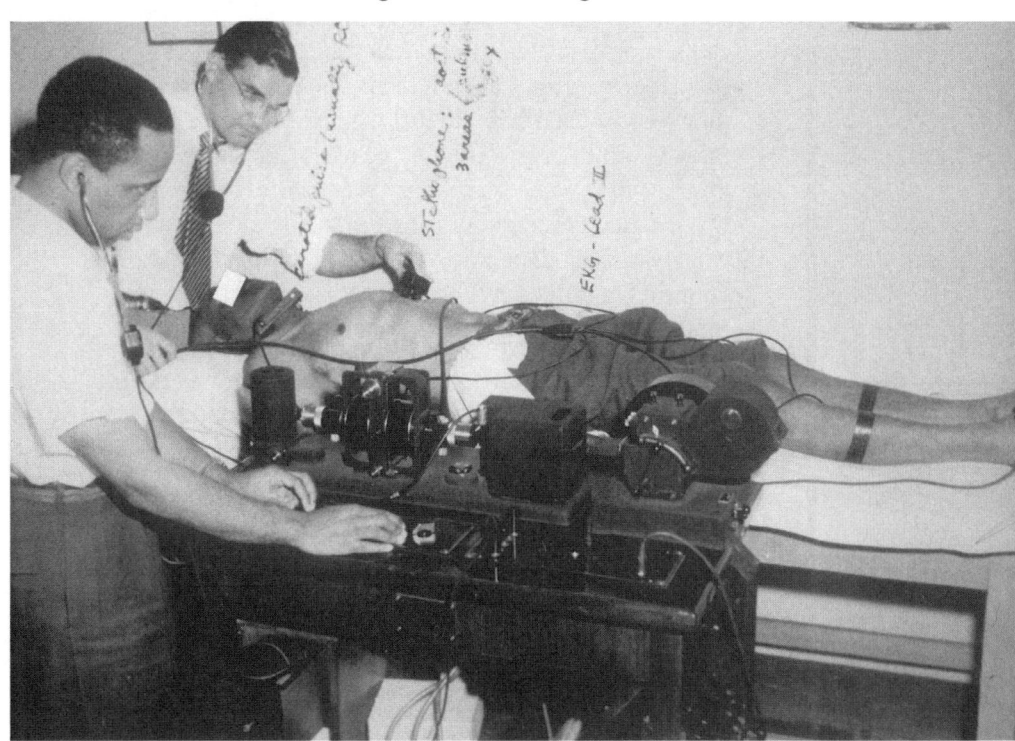

to treat the men was immoral. He also realized that the study violated ethical standards for medical research involving humans that had been established by the Nuremberg Code two decades earlier. On November 9, 1966, Buxton wrote to Dr. William J. Brown, director of the PHS Division of Venereal Diseases. Buxton

A Man of Conscience

When former investigator Peter Buxton testified in 1973 before a congressional committee investigating the Tuskegee study, he explained why he acted to stop the controversial research project. He was questioned by Senator Edward Kennedy of Massachusetts. His testimony can be found in Reverby's *Tuskegee's Truths*.

Senator Kennedy: What bothered you most about the study?

Mr. Buxton: The fact that the participants really did not seem to be consulted. They were being used. It was difficult for me to tell really what was going on from [reading past reports on the study]. It seemed apparent to me that these people had been told that they had a disease and that they could receive some benefits as they did some things, and in some sort of hazy way their cooperation was induced. I do not use the word "consent." I felt that what was being done was very close to murder and was, if you will, an institutionalized form of murder and something the Public Health Service should have no part of.

Senator Kennedy: Why do you think there was such reluctance [in 1972] for others in the [government] to move on this issue. This is not 1932 or 1934.

Mr. Buxton: Sir, I feel that it had become an accepted thing within the Public Health Service. Oh yes, so and so over in that office is working on Tuskegee, and here is some data that we got, and nobody paid any attention to it for years. It was just an ongoing thing, not subject to any review.

argued that the study was unethical because doctors had lied to the men about their illness and had not told them they were part of a medical study. Buxton later said of his letter, "I pointed out that the Tuskegee Study could be compared to the German medical 'experiments' at Dachau [a concentration camp] and that public disclosure of such a scandal could jeopardize Congressional funding for other, beneficial PHS projects."[77]

"Political Dynamite"

Buxton was invited several months later to a government seminar on syphilis in Atlanta, Georgia, where he met with Brown and Dr. John Cutler, a PHS official who was an expert on the study. Instead of discussing with Buxton the issues he had raised, the two doctors berated him for criticizing a project that was providing what they claimed was valuable knowledge about syphilis. Buxton, however, stood up to the verbal assault. He insisted again that the study was wrong because the men were being used for medical research without their consent, a violation of medical ethics that the U.S. government had promised to honor in adopting the Nuremberg Code and signing the Declaration of Helsinki.

After returning to San Francisco, Buxton heard nothing more about his complaints. He worked for the PHS clinic there until November 1967, when he resigned to attend law school. But the study still bothered him. So in November 1968, Buxton wrote to Brown to express once more his grave doubts about the study's morality and to plead that the ill men be treated.

This time Buxton offered another reason to end the study—the fact that all the men were black, which he claimed imparted serious racial overtones to the project. When the Tuskegee study had begun in 1932, blacks were being denied many of their civil rights, especially in the South. In the 1960s, however, African Americans were fighting fiercely to win those rights and to correct injustices that they had endured for centuries. Buxton said that many people, not just blacks, would brand the study racist because it had taken advantage of uneducated blacks for the purpose of scientific research. He wrote: "The group is 100 percent Negro. This in itself is political dynamite. [Today] it would be morally unethical to begin such a study with such a group [because it seemed based solely on race]."[78]

PHS Denial

Buxton's second letter finally forced PHS officials to reconsider the study. On December 16, 1968, Brown wrote to Buxton that a special committee would evaluate the issues he had raised. This group, meeting in Atlanta on February 6, 1969, was chaired by Dr. David Sencer, who headed the Communicable Disease Center, which in the past had been known as the PHS Division of Venereal Diseases. The committee members included federal and state health officials, representatives of several medical schools, other medical experts, and representatives from the Milbank Memorial Fund, which had been providing money for autopsies and funeral expenses since the study's early years.

The meeting began with a presentation of a history of the study, including the fact that fifty-six men with syphilis and thirty-six controls were still living; those survivors ranged in age from fifty-nine to eighty-five. When Sencer asked the group if the study should be ended, a long debate ensued.

Most of those present supported continuing the project, claiming that it was yielding important information on syphilis. "You will never have another study like this: take advantage of it,"[79] argued Dr. J. Lawton Smith of the University of Miami. Because penicillin could now easily cure syphilis, Smith said there would never again be a chance to study a large group of men suffering the long-term effects of untreated syphilis. Smith believed that knowledge outweighed any harm being done to the men.

Dr. Gene Stollerman of the University of Tennessee, however, forcefully argued that it was morally wrong not to treat the men for the disease they had. He also warned that if they were not treated and the study became known to the general public, the federal agency would be heavily criticized for violating the men's rights. Stollerman argued that the criticism and corresponding loss of prestige could hurt the agency's ability to perform its other duties in safeguarding public health.

After much debate, the committee decided to continue the study in order to keep learning about syphilis. The committee considered telling the men about the research aims of the project so they could give their consent to be part of it. But the members rejected that proposal, mainly because most of them believed that

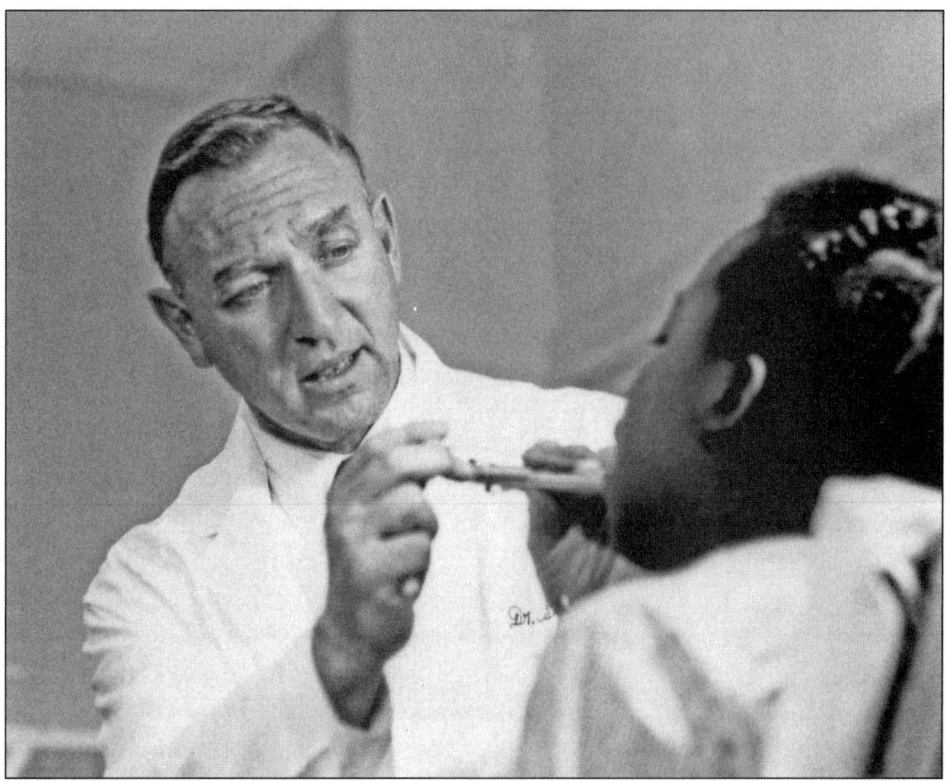

Dr. Gene Stollerman (left) investigated the Tuskegee study's ethics violations in 1968. He concluded that depriving subjects of proper treatment was altogether immoral.

the participants were neither smart enough nor educated enough to understand the study or realize its significance.

On February 27, Brown wrote Buxton to explain that the study would go on: "After an examination of the data and a very lengthy discussion regarding treatment, our committee of highly competent professionals did not agree nor recommend that the study group be treated."[80]

The Story Is Told

Once again, PHS officials had decided to ignore criticism of the Tuskegee study. Believing there was nothing more he could do, Buxton resumed his law classes. But because the study continued to haunt him, he kept talking about it to people he met in hopes of discovering a way to help the men. In July 1972 Buxton finally found a person who could do something: Edith Lederer, a reporter for the worldwide news organization the Associated Press (AP).

Lederer took the information about the study to her editors. They assigned the story to Jean Heller, an investigative reporter in AP's Washington, D.C., office. In that city, Heller researched the facts of the study and interviewed government officials. On July 25, 1972, Heller's story on the Tuskegee study appeared on the front page of the *Washington Star*, and in the next few days it also ran in many other newspapers around the country and the world. This is how Heller began her story: "For 40 years the United States Public Health Service has conducted a study in which human beings with syphilis, who were induced to serve as guinea pigs, have gone without medical treatment for the disease [even] though an effective therapy [penicillin] was eventually discovered."[81]

Reaction

Heller's story created a firestorm of controversy. People from all walks of life were outraged. Top government officials who had been unaware of the study's existence condemned it. People in the United States and countries around the world were appalled that the doctors had misled the men for so many years and endangered their lives by not treating them for the serious disease.

Dr. Donald Printz of the Centers for Disease Control's Venereal Disease Branch stated that the study was "almost like genocide [mass murder],"[82] and Dr. Merlin K. Duval, assistant secretary of the Department of Health, Education, and Welfare, promised an investigation. Admitting that he was "shocked and horrified," Duval said the most important question to be answered was "why the study was permitted to continue past the time when penicillin became the effective choice against the disease."[83]

The reaction of the news media was no less harsh. Television news anchor Harry Reasoner concluded that the experiment "used human beings as laboratory animals in a long and inefficient study of how long it takes syphilis to kill someone."[84] With similar outrage, the *St. Louis Post-Dispatch* newspaper stated, "The immorality of the experiment was inherent in its premise [not to treat sick people]."[85]

"I Don't Know What They Used Us For"

When the truth was finally revealed to the subjects of the study, the men were intensely confused. Carter Howard, one of the men in the control group, admitted that during all those years, "I didn't know what they meant [about 'bad blood'] or what they wanted."[86] In addition to never having been told that they were part of a long-term medical study, the uneducated men had trouble even understanding the concept of the kind of medical research they had unwittingly taken part in. When one man in the study was told that he and the others had been used as "guinea pigs," the small animals often used in medical experiments, he confessed, "I don't know what [guinea pig] means. I don't know what they used us for."[87]

It was also a shock for the men to learn about the study from newspaper headlines and reporters who contacted them for their reaction. Charles Pollard was at a stockyard selling some cattle when a reporter tracked him down and told him the truth about the study. "I was surprised,"[88] Pollard admitted.

These residents of Davisville in Macon County were among the subjects in the Tuskegee study. The fact that all of the subjects were black led most people to condemn the study as racist.

The fact that all the men in the study were African Americans made most people believe the study was racist. One such person was civil rights attorney Fred D. Gray. "Those selected," he said, "were [chosen] solely because of their race and color in violation of their rights."[89] Many people believed that the government would never have used whites in such experiments, but was able to use blacks because the racism that existed when the study began made the men politically and economically powerless.

Massachusetts senator Edward Kennedy chaired the congressional subcommittee that investigated the civil rights and medical ethics abuses of the Tuskegee study.

Government Action

The reaction to the story was so overwhelmingly negative and powerful that Duval on August 24 appointed nine people, all of them doctors, to look into the matter. Five of the nine were black, including the group's head, Dillard University president Broadus Nathaniel Butler. In October 1972 what was called the Tuskegee Syphilis Study Ad Hoc Advisory Panel advised the government to stop the study. In November the federal government officially ended it.

In its final report, issued on April 28, 1973, the panel condemned the study as "ethically unjustified." It said that the men with syphilis should have been treated with penicillin when it became available and that the men should have been told what the study was about and what risks they faced.

The report was only part of the U.S. government's response. In February and March 1973, the Congressional Subcommittee on Health, chaired by Senator Edward Kennedy, held a series of hearings on the Tuskegee study. When Kennedy asked one of the men, Lester Scott, how he felt about having participated in the study, he answered: "I don't think much of it. They were just using us for something else—for an experiment. If they had told me [I had syphilis], I would have gone to a family doctor and got treated."[90]

"To Choose What Shall or Shall Not Happen"

The hearings provided the impetus for a national review of the ethics involved in experiments using human subjects and led to new federal regulations to protect participants in such studies. Congress in 1974 created the National Commission for the Protection of Human Subjects of Biomedical and Behavioral Research. The commission created ethical guidelines for such studies that continue to govern medical research today. Chief among the requirements the commission imposed is that people taking part in such a study must give their "informed consent"; this means that test subjects agree to take part only after being told about all aspects of the study, including any dangers to their health.

On April 18, 1979, the commission issued the "Belmont Report," which further refined and strengthened federal human research guidelines. The document said that medical researchers must respect several basic rights of men and women involved in medical studies. The most important right is this one:

> [In] research involving human subjects, respect for persons demands that subjects enter into the research voluntarily and with adequate information [and] subjects, to the degree that they are capable, be given the opportunity to choose what shall or shall not happen to them.[91]

Helping the Men

Once the government ended the study, federal officials decided to offer medical aid to the survivors to make up for what they had gone through. Whether motivated by a sense of guilt or a sincere desire to help the men, officials in April 1973 announced that the government would provide free health care to the survivors of the study for the rest of their lives. The officials also said that the men's families would still receive funeral payments when they died, even though families would no longer have to authorize autopsies for their loved ones. Two years later, the government extended the health care to include any of the men's wives and children who had contracted syphilis during the study.

The study's survivors, however, believed that they were owed more than belated medical care. When Lester Scott testified before a congressional hearing in March 1973, he told Senator Kennedy, "They ought to give us compensation."[92] As Scott was making that statement, attorney Fred D. Gray was already working to get the men in the study the financial award they believed they deserved.

Gray had long been active in the civil rights movement and was experienced in arguing on behalf of those whose rights had been violated. Yet, although Gray had lived in Tuskegee for many years and been active in winning rights for local blacks, he had never heard of the study before reading Heller's newspaper story. He wrote of his surprise: "It was astounding to me that such a study could have [been kept secret] for forty years. I was shocked but I was hardly surprised. I had witnessed many areas where African Americans had been treated unjustly. This case was especially appalling because it was officially sanctioned by the federal government."[93]

The legal action on behalf of the men began on July 27, 1972, when Charles Pollard walked into Gray's office. Pollard said that he was one of the men in the study and felt he had been wronged. Pollard thought Gray could help him because of his reputation for fighting for black civil rights. On July 24, 1973, after researching the case and contacting the survivors of the study as well as relatives of the men who had died, Gray filed a $1.8 billion lawsuit against the federal government on behalf of all the men in the study. The suit sought financial compensation for the damage the disease had done to them and their families.

The suit, however, never went to trial. In December 1974 the federal government agreed in an out-of-court settlement to pay $10 million in damages to more than six thousand people. Sur-

A renowned champion of black civil rights, attorney Fred Gray filed a lawsuit in 1973 on behalf of the Tuskegee study subjects against the federal government.

vivors of the study who had had syphilis received $37,500 in damages, survivors of the control group received $16,000, and descendants of participants who had died received smaller sums.

Finally, an Apology

Despite the money the federal government had given them, many of the survivors—as well as other African Americans—were upset that the government never actually said it was sorry for what it had done to the men. In 1996 the Legacy Committee was formed to pressure federal officials for an apology. The committee, made up of historians, educators, and medical professionals, many of them African American, recommended that President Bill Clinton formally apologize to the men. As study survivor Herman Shaw explained, "We suffered through it, and we want to be recognized. And I think that we as people should be recognized."[94]

On May 16, 1997, sixty-five years after the study began, Shaw and the other survivors finally got their apology. In a ceremony in the East Wing of the White House attended by five of the eight

A President Apologizes

On May 16, 1997, President Bill Clinton formally apologized for the Tuskegee Study of Untreated Syphilis in the Negro Male. When the president made his remarks in a ceremony in the East Wing of the White House in Washington, D.C., five of the eight surviving participants in the study were in the audience—Herman Shaw, Charles Pollard, Carter Howard, Fred Simmons, and Frederick Moss. This excerpt from Clinton's speech is from the National Archives and Records Administration Web site:

> The United States government did something that was wrong—deeply, profoundly, morally wrong. It was an outrage to our commitment to integrity and equality for all our citizens. To the survivors, to the wives and family members, the children and the grandchildren, I say what you know: No power on Earth can give you back the lives lost, the pain suffered, the years of internal torment and anguish. What was done cannot be undone. But we can end the silence. We can stop turning our heads away. We can look at you in the eye and finally say on behalf of the American people, what the United States government did was shameful, and I am sorry.

The president's remarks were met with applause, long and loud, from those assembled.

President Bill Clinton greets Tuskegee study survivor Herman Shaw at the White House in 1997.

surviving participants of the Tuskegee study, President Clinton expressed the nation's regret for what the federal government had done:

> To our African American citizens, I am sorry that your federal government orchestrated a study so clearly racist. . . . The American people are sorry—for the loss [of life and health], for the years of hurt. You did nothing wrong, but you were grievously wronged. I apologize and I am sorry that this apology has been so long in coming.[95]

Shaw, who was ninety-five, was chosen to speak for the men in the study. He said he was grateful to the president "for doing your best to right this tragic wrong, and resolving that America should never again allow such an event to occur."[96]

A Lack of Remorse

President Clinton's apology to the men in the Tuskegee study finally put the federal government on record as being sorry for what had happened. However, many of those who conducted the study never showed any remorse over what they had done and continued to defend the study long after it was exposed. Two decades after the study was made public, Dr. John Cutler, who had worked on the study in the 1940s and 1950s, still did not think he and the other doctors had done anything wrong. Cutler said: "Tuskegee was undertaken for the highest ethical reasons. We had the responsibility, the job had to be done, and we did it."[97]

Cutler and some other doctors believed they had acted correctly in running the study. In any case, none of them were ever charged with any crimes for the parts they played in the research. Some officials, however, did come to regret their participation in the infamous study. Dr. Sidney Olansky once said, "I'm sorry I was involved in it, even though I didn't start it and I didn't finish it. I'm terribly sorry. I wish it had never started. It didn't accomplish any of the things I wanted it to or thought it might. Sure I'm sorry. It has cost me a great deal."[98] After Olansky's name surfaced in a 1992 television documentary about the study, friends and patients he had treated for years were horrified to learn about his

Herman Shaw, a Survivor of the Study

—————◼—————

When President Clinton apologized for the Tuskegee study, he was introduced by Herman Shaw, one of the study's survivors. Shaw explained to the audience why the apology was so important. His words are taken from *The Tuskegee Syphilis Study: The Real Story and Beyond*, by Fred D. Gray.

> We were treated unfairly and to some extent like guinea pigs. We were not pigs. We were all hard working men, not boys, and citizens of the United States. The wounds that were inflicted upon us cannot be undone. I am saddened to think of those who did not survive and whose families will forever live with the knowledge that their death and suffering was preventable. . . . This ceremony is important because the damage done by the Tuskegee Study is much deeper than the wounds any of us may have suffered. It speaks to our faith in government and the ability of medical science to serve as a force for good. [But in] my opinion, it is never too late to work to restore faith and trust.

involvement. Many of them harshly criticized Olansky for his participation.

At least one PHS worker was truly sorry about what happened to the men in the Tuskegee study. Although her loyalty to the project was so strong that she defended it for years after it became known to the public, Eunice Rivers finally realized that the study was wrong because it had endangered the men's health. "We should have told them they had syphilis," she finally admitted. "And we should have given them penicillin."[99]

"America's Metaphor for Racism"

The Tuskegee study today is universally condemned because doctors believed that what they would learn in their research project was more important than saving the lives of the men they were studying. Most people also feel it was immoral because the project involved only blacks. Historian Susan M. Reverby edited *Tuskegee's Truths: Rethinking the Tuskegee Syphilis Study*, a collection

And so, a quarter century after the Study ended, President Clinton's decision to gather us here, to allow us to finally put this horrible nightmare behind us as a nation, is a most welcomed decision. In order for America to reach its full potential we must truly be one America—black, red, and white together; trusting each other, caring for each other, and never allowing the kind of tragedy which happened to us in the Tuskegee Study to ever occur again.

Herman Shaw lived to hear President Clinton's apology for the federal government's role in the Tuskegee study.

of original documents, interviews, and articles on the study. In her introduction to the book, Reverby wrote that people today need to remember the study so that something similar never happens again:

> The Tuskegee study is America's metaphor for racism in medical research. It is often paired with the Nazi doctors' experiments on Holocaust victims [during World War II]. Both serve as reminders of what medicine aligned with state power can do to those defined as "other." The story of the Tuskegee study is a form of collective trauma because it was caused by human hands, it affected an entire community, and it continues to haunt us.[100]

The Tuskegee Study's Twin Legacies

When Ernest Hendon died on January 16, 2004, the Tuskegee Study of Untreated Syphilis in the Negro Male finally came to the natural conclusion that its originators had envisioned for it: Of the six hundred black men who had been chosen for the study seven decades earlier, Hendon was the last to die. Hendon, who was ninety-six years old, died in a hospital in Opelinka, Alabama, of natural causes.

But even the death of the last participant in a research project begun in 1932 could not truly end the Tuskegee study. Like many events of the past, the study continues to shape events today through the twin legacies it left behind, one good and one bad.

"Never Again"

The positive legacy of the Tuskegee study is that the rights of people involved in medical research have been greatly strengthened so that the injustices committed during the study never occur again. Today's medical researchers are committed to honoring the new ethical codes regarding human experimentation that developed in the last half of the twentieth century. And medical personnel are now educated about the need to follow these new ethical standards.

An important step toward achieving this goal came on May 15, 1999, with the opening of the Tuskegee University National Center for Bioethics in Research and Health. As part of the nation's formal apology for the study in 1997, President Clinton awarded the school a $200,000 grant to begin planning the center. Today the educational facility trains African American medical personnel in medical ethics and explores moral issues involved in research projects.

The training in medical ethics that students now receive at Tuskegee University is in sharp contrast to the abuses practiced

Alabama's Tuskegee Institute, the site of the notorious syphilis study, now houses the Tuskegee University National Center for Bioethics in Research and Health.

there decades ago in the Tuskegee study. This training is a powerful symbol of the significant changes that have taken place in both medical research and race relations in America since the study ended. In 1997 Benjamin F. Paxton, president of Tuskegee University, explained why the bioethics center is important: "We must never again permit a Nazi-like experiment on human beings to take place and go unchallenged for so long. If we just get an apology that says I'm sorry, we have not gained very much. We must have people [in the medical profession] speaking with knowledge, because knowledge is power."[101]

Distrust of the Government

Knowledge, however, is often a double-edged sword. Knowing how the Tuskegee study abused the rights of the black participants, many African Americans today fear or distrust a medical establishment they believe to be racist because most of its personnel are white. That is the second, negative legacy of the study. According to Dr. Vanessa Northington Gamble, an African American medical historian, the study even today evokes fears that African Americans have about medical care:

> The Tuskegee Syphilis Study continues to cast its shadow over the lives of African-Americans. For many black people, it has come to represent the racism that pervades American institutions and the disdain in which black lives are often held. It is a powerful metaphor in our community [that] has come to represent why we should not trust our doctor. It has come to represent why we should not trust the government.[102]

Public health experts say that this attitude continues to have serious consequences for black Americans. In February 2003 J. Lawrence Miller, executive director of the Black Educational AIDS Project in Baltimore, claimed that what he calls the "Tuskegee mentality" hinders efforts to get blacks to participate in research projects to test new drugs for AIDS even though many blacks have the disease: "That distrust [of the medical profession] has become cultural. How do you fight culture? You can't, except for education."[103]

That distrust is fueled in part by myths and rumors that exaggerate and distort the facts of the Tuskegee study. For example, rumors persist that white doctors intentionally infected study participants with syphilis. Although this is false, it undoubtedly influenced the 10 percent of blacks who in a 1990 survey said that they believed the U.S. government created AIDS and the 20 percent who thought that such a theory was at least a possibility.

Echoes of Tuskegee

This distorted perception of the medical profession and the government was strengthened in a strange way in 2003 when Marvel comics published a series titled Truth: Red, White & Black. The comic book revived a popular 1940s comic book superhero named Captain America, a World War II soldier who receives fantastic powers when military doctors inject him with a "super soldier" serum. In the new comic book series, the serum is tested on blacks before being given to Captain America. And because the serum had not been perfected, many of the blacks die or become horribly deformed.

Although a work of fiction, the Truth series evokes the very real racial oppression that existed during the war years. And the legacy of distrust that the Tuskegee study created makes the comic book's unlikely premise seem possible. In reviewing the series for *Nation* magazine, Alan Jenkins wrote:

> The story line draws its inspiration, and its believability, from the notorious Tuskegee experiments. With its echoes of Tuskegee, the Truth series asks and answers the question: If the US military had to test a dangerous new formula on World War II GIs, would it experiment on blond, blue-eyed Steve Rogers [the original soldier in the Captain America series], or anonymous African-Americans?[104]

The comic book series is a work of fantasy, but it is still easy for many African Americans and other U.S. citizens to believe that the government could have done something like that to black soldiers. Because the federal government once allowed hundreds of black men with syphilis to go untreated for four decades for the sake of a scientific experiment, it is not hard for many people to believe that the government might use blacks to test a new super serum so that a white person would not have to suffer.

A Moral Failure

The Tuskegee study has made many African Americans lose trust in the medical profession because they consider it a racist project that abused the rights of blacks. However, the actions of the doctors in the study involves a moral failure that extends far beyond race.

When the Tuskegee study began in 1932, doctors like Raymond Vonderlehr believed that the information it would yield was more valuable than the lives of the men it would study but fail to treat for the serious disease they had. In his formal apology on May 16, 1997, President Clinton noted that the doctors who ran the study were guilty of turning their backs on the most sacred duty a physician has. Said Clinton: "The people who ran the study at Tuskegee diminished the stature of man by abandoning the most basic ethical precepts. They forgot their pledge to heal and repair. They had the power to heal the survivors and all the others and they did not."[105]

Notes

Introduction:
A Case of Medical Racism

1. Quoted in Indiana University, "Factual Basis: An Historical Look at the Tuskegee Study," 2001. www.indiana.edu/~poynter/sas/lb/facts.html.
2. Quoted in Vanessa Northington Gamble, "Tuskegee Lessons: Syphilis Study Leaves Behind Legacy of Mistrust," National Public Radio, July 25, 2002. www.npr.org/programs/morning/features/2002/jul/tuskegee/commentary.
3. Quoted in James H. Jones, *Bad Blood: The Tuskegee Syphilis Experiment.* New York: Free Press, 1993, p. 5.
4. Fred D. Gray, *The Tuskegee Syphilis Study: The Real Story and Beyond.* Montgomery, AL: Black Belt, 1998, p. 105.
5. Gray, *The Tuskegee Syphilis Study*, p. 105.
6. Vanessa Northington Gamble, "Under the Shadow of Tuskegee: African Americans and Health Care," *American Journal of Public Health*, November 1997, pp. 1776, 1783.

Chapter 1:
Roots of the Tuskegee Study

7. Quoted in Jones, *Bad Blood*, p. 54.

8. Quoted in Jones, *Bad Blood*, p. 57.
9. Quoted in Thomas Parran, *Shadow on the Land: Syphilis, the White Man's Burden.* New York: Waverly, 1937, p. 168.
10. Quoted in Allan M. Brandt, "The Case of the Tuskegee Syphilis Experiment," *Hastings Center Report* 8, December 1978, p. 21.
11. Quoted in Thomas G. Benedek and Jonathon Erlen, "The Scientific Environment of the Tuskegee Study of Syphilis," *Perspectives in Biology and Medicine*, Autumn 1999, p. 1.
12. Andrew Goliszek, *In the Name of Science: A History of Secret Programs, Medical Research, and Human Experimentation.* New York: St. Martin's, 2003, p. 17.
13. Parran, *Shadow on the Land*, p. 165.
14. Robert J. Norrell, *Reaping the Whirlwind: The Civil Rights Movement in Tuskegee.* New York: Knopf, 1985, p. 23.
15. Parran, *Shadow on the Land*, p. 172.
16. Parran, *Shadow on the Land*, p. 173.
17. Parran, *Shadow on the Land*, p. 168.
18. Quoted in David L. Kirp, "Blood, Sweat, and Tears: The Tuskegee Experiment and the Era of AIDS," *Tikkun*, May/June 1995, p. 50.
19. Quoted in Susan M. Reverby, ed., *Tuskegee's Truths: Rethinking the*

Tuskegee Syphilis Study. Chapel Hill: University of North Carolina Press, 2000, p. 241.

Chapter 2:
The Tuskegee Study Is Born

20. Quoted in Stephen B. Thomas and Sandra Crouse Quinn, "The Tuskegee Syphilis Study, 1932 to 1972: Implications for HIV Education and AIDS Risk Education Programs in the Black Community," *American Journal of Public Health*, November 1991, p. 1500.

21. Quoted in A.W. Fourtner, C.R. Fourtner, and C.F. Herreid, "'Bad Blood': A Case Study of the Tuskegee Syphilis Project." http://ublib.buffalo.edu/libraries/projects/cases/blood.

22. Quoted in Reverby, *Tuskegee's Truths*, p. 77.

23. Quoted in Stephen Chau and Thomas Liu, "Prejudice in Health Care." www.stanford.edu/class/e297c/poverty_prejudice/slavery_colonialism_reparations/chauliu.

24. Quoted in Brandt, "The Case of the Tuskegee Syphilis Experiment," p. 21.

25. Quoted in Goliszek, *In the Name of Science*, p. 81.

26. Quoted in Michigan State University, "Faces of Tuskegee." www.msu.edu/course/hm/546/tuskegee.htm.

27. Quoted in *Economist*, "Don't Let It Happen Again," May 17, 1997, p. 27.

28. Quoted in Goliszek, *In the Name of Science*, p. 80.

29. Gray, *The Tuskegee Syphilis Study*, p. 35.

30. Quoted in Gray, *The Tuskegee Syphilis Study*, p. 54.

31. Quoted in Reverby, *Tuskegee's Truths*, p. 83.

32. Quoted in Susan M. Reverby, "History of an Apology: From Tuskegee to the White House," *Research Nurse*, vol. 3, no. 4, 1997, p. 1.

33. Quoted in Stephen B. Thomas, "The Legacy of Tuskegee," *Body Positive*, February 2000, p. 62.

Chapter 3: The Tuskegee
Study Continues for Decades

34. Quoted in Jones, *Bad Blood*, p. 114.

35. Quoted in Reverby, *Tuskegee's Truths*, p. 138.

36. Quoted in Jim Auchmutey, "Ghosts of Tuskegee," *Atlanta Journal and Constitution*, September 6, 1992, p. M1.

37. Quoted in Reverby *Tuskegee's Truths*, p. 138.

38. Quoted in Gray, *The Tuskegee Syphilis Study*, p. 51.

39. Quoted in Auchmutey, "Ghosts of Tuskegee," p. M1.

40. Eunice Rivers, Stanley H. Schuman, Lloyd Simpson, and Sidney Olansky, "Twenty Years of Followup Experience in a Long-Range Medical Study," *Public Health Reports*, April 1953, p. 391.

41. Quoted in Gray, *The Tuskegee Syphilis Study*, p. 59.

42. Quoted in *Jacksonville (Florida) Free Press*, "Black History Month 2001: The Tuskegee Experiment," February 21, 2001, p. 2.

43. Quoted in Brandt, "The Case of the Tuskegee Syphilis Experiment," p. 21.

44. Rivers et al., "Twenty Years of Followup Experience in a Long-Range Medical Study," p. 391.
45. Rivers et al., "Twenty Years of Followup Experience in a Long-Range Medical Study," p. 391.
46. Quoted in Reverby, "History of an Apology," p. 1.
47. Quoted in Jones, *Bad Blood*, p. 151.
48. Quoted in Jones, *Bad Blood*, p. 154.
49. Quoted in Reverby, *Tuskegee's Truths*, p. 77.
50. Quoted in Jones, *Bad Blood*, p. 161.
51. Gray, *The Tuskegee Syphilis Study*, p. 85.
52. Quoted in Reverby, *Tuskegee's Truths*, p. 356.
53. Quoted in Jones, *Bad Blood*, p. 158.
54. Quoted in Reverby, *Tuskegee's Truths*, p. 360.
55. Quoted in Reverby, *Tuskegee's Truths*, p. 24.
56. Quoted in Jones, *Bad Blood*, p. 177.
57. Quoted in Reverby, *Tuskegee's Truths*, p. 355.
58. Quoted in Jones, *Bad Blood*, p. 130.
59. Quoted in Reverby, *Tuskegee's Truths*, p. 124.
60. Quoted in Jones, *Bad Blood*, p. 112.

Chapter 4:
Questions and Problems Arise

61. Quoted in Jones, *Bad Blood*, p. 139.
62. Jones, *Bad Blood*, p. 173.
63. Quoted in Reverby, *Tuskegee's Truths*, p. 89.
64. Reverby, "History of an Apology," p. 1.
65. Quoted in Indiana University, "Factual Basis."
66. Quoted in Thomas and Quinn, "The Tuskegee Syphilis Study, 1932 to 1972," p. 1501.
67. Quoted in Indiana University, "Factual Basis."
68. Quoted in Borgna Brunner, "The Tuskegee Syphilis Experiment," 2003. www.tuskegee.edu/Global/Story.asp?s=1207586.
69. Quoted in *News Hour with Jim Lehrer*, "An Apology 65 Years Late," May 16, 1997. www.pbs.org/news hour/bb/health/may97/tuskegee_5-16.html.
70. Quoted in World Medical Association, "Declaration of Helsinki," 1964. www.wma.net/e/policy/b3.htm.
71. Quoted in Jones, *Bad Blood*, p. 180.
72. Quoted in Auchmutey, "Ghosts of Tuskegee," p. M1.
73. Quoted in Auchmutey, "Ghosts of Tuskegee," p. M1.
74. Quoted in Jones, *Bad Blood*, p. 190.
75. Quoted in Reverby, *Tuskegee's Truths*, p. 107.
76. Quoted in Reverby, *Tuskegee's Truths*, p. 98.

Chapter 5: The Tuskegee Study: A National Scandal

77. Quoted in Gray, *The Tuskegee Syphilis Study*, p. 76.
78. Quoted in Jones, *Bad Blood*, p. 193.
79. Quoted in Gray, *The Tuskegee Syphilis Study*, p. 69.
80. Quoted in Reverby, *Tuskegee's Truths*, p. 154.
81. Quoted in Reverby, *Tuskegee's Truths*, p. 116.
82. Quoted in Thomas and Quinn, "The Tuskegee Syphilis Study, 1932 to 1972," p. 1502.

83. Quoted in Jones, *Bad Blood*, p. 206.

84. Quoted in Brunner, "The Tuskegee Syphilis Experiment."

85. Quoted in Chau and Liu, "Prejudice in Health Care."

86. Quoted in Auchmutey, "Ghosts of Tuskegee," p. M1.

87. Quoted in Jones, *Bad Blood*, p. 219.

88. Quoted in Reverby, *Tuskegee's Truths*, p. 140.

89. Gray, *The Tuskegee Syphilis Study*, p. 105.

90. Quoted in Gray, *The Tuskegee Syphilis Study*, p. 102.

91. National Commission for the Protection of Human Subjects of Biomedical and Behavioral Research, "Belmont Report," April 18, 1979. http://ohsr.od.nih.gov/guidelines/belmont.html.

92. Quoted in Reverby, *Tuskegee's Truths*, p. 142.

93. Gray, *The Tuskegee Syphilis Study*, p. 24.

94. Quoted in *News Hour with Jim Lehrer*, "An Apology 65 Years Late."

95. Bill Clinton, "Apology for Study Done in Tuskegee," May 16, 1997. www.clinton4.nara.gov/textonly/New/Remarks/Fri/19970516-898.html.

96. Quoted in Gray, *The Tuskegee Syphilis Study*, p. 162.

97. Quoted in Auchmutey, "Ghosts of Tuskegee," p. M1.

98. Quoted in Reverby, *Tuskegee's Truths*, p. 523.

99. Quoted in Auchmutey, "Ghosts of Tuskegee," p. M1.

100. Reverby, *Tuskegee's Truths*, p. 3.

Epilogue: The Tuskegee Study's Twin Legacies

101. Quoted in Joan H. Allen, "Survivor: Tuskegee Experiment Was Racist, Nazi-Like," *New York Amsterdam News*, May 31, 1997, p. 15.

102. Quoted in E.R. Shipp, "Sadly, Use of Unwitting Blacks as Laboratory Animals Is an Old Story," *New York Daily News*, May 19, 1997, p. 1.

103. Quoted in Deborah Kong, "Tuskegee Memories Keep Blacks Wary About Studies," *Houston Chronicle*, February 26, 2003, p. 11.

104. Alan Jenkins, "Truth: Red, White & Black," *Nation*, May 12, 2003, p. 36.

105. Clinton, "Apology for Study Done in Tuskegee."

For Further Reading

Books

Fred D. Gray, *The Tuskegee Syphilis Study: The Real Story and Beyond.* Montgomery, AL: Black Belt, 1998. This famous civil rights attorney, who filed a lawsuit on behalf of the men in the Tuskegee study, provides a solid history of the study.

James H. Jones, *Bad Blood: The Tuskegee Syphilis Experiment.* New York: Free Press, 1993. This is considered the best book ever written about the study.

Susan M. Reverby, ed., *Tuskegee's Truths: Rethinking the Tuskegee Syphilis Study.* Chapel Hill: University of North Carolina Press, 2000. Includes historical documents as well as a wide array of articles and excerpts from books about the Tuskegee study. This book is an invaluable aid in understanding the study.

Web Sites

Centers for Disease Control and Prevention (www.cdc.gov). The Web site for the federal government agency responsible for monitoring American health has information about syphilis and the Tuskegee study.

Tuskegee University (www.tuskegee.edu). The university's Web site has some interesting articles and information on the Tuskegee study.

University of Virginia (www.health system.virginia.edu/internet/library/). The university's health sciences library's Web site can be searched for details of the history of the Tuskegee study and presents the apology by President Clinton.

Works Consulted

Books

Andrew Goliszek, *In the Name of Science: A History of Secret Programs, Medical Research, and Human Experimentation.* New York: St. Martin's, 2003. Identifies many medical studies and experiments that often ignored medical ethics.

Robert J. Norrell, *Reaping the Whirlwind: The Civil Rights Movement in Tuskegee.* New York: Knopf, 1985. A look at how the fight for civil rights affected Tuskegee.

Thomas Parran, *Shadow on the Land: Syphilis, the White Man's Burden.* New York: Waverly, 1937. Parran was the U.S. surgeon general when this book was published and director of the Public Health Service Division of Venereal Diseases before that. The book, which includes a chapter on the Tuskegee study, is interesting because it shows the attitudes doctors had then toward both syphilis and African Americans.

Periodicals

Joan H. Allen, "Survivor: Tuskegee Experiment Was Racist, Nazi-Like," *New York Amsterdam News*, May 31, 1997.

Jim Auchmutey, "Ghosts of Tuskegee," *Atlanta Journal and Constitution*, September 6, 1992.

Thomas G. Benedek and Jonathon Erlen,

"The Scientific Environment of the Tuskegee Study of Syphilis," *Perspectives in Biology and Medicine*, Autumn 1999.

Allan M. Brandt, "The Case of the Tuskegee Syphilis Experiment," *Hastings Center Report 8*, December 1978.

Economist, "Don't Let It Happen Again," May 17, 1997.

Vanessa Northington Gamble, "Under the Shadow of Tuskegee: African Americans and Health Care," *American Journal of Public Health*, November 1997.

Jacksonville (Florida) Free Press, "Black History Month 2001: The Tuskegee Experiment," February 21, 2001.

Alan Jenkins, "Truth: Red, White & Black," *Nation*, May 12, 2003.

David L. Kirp, "Blood, Sweat, and Tears: The Tuskegee Experiment and the Era of AIDS," *Tikkun*, May/June 1995.

Deborah Kong, "Tuskegee Memories Keep Blacks Wary About Studies," *Houston Chronicle*, February 26, 2003.

Dennis McLellan, "Ernest Hendon, 96; Tuskegee Syphilis Study's Last Survivor," *Los Angeles Times*, January 25, 2004.

Susan M. Reverby, "History of an Apology: From Tuskegee to the White

House," *Research Nurse*, vol. 3, no. 4, 1997.

Eunice Rivers, Stanley H. Schuman, Lloyd Simpson, and Sidney Olansky, "Twenty Years of Followup Experience in a Long-Range Medical Study," *Public Health Reports*, April 1953.

E.R. Shipp, "Sadly, Use of Unwitting Blacks as Laboratory Animals Is an Old Story," *New York Daily News*, May 19, 1997.

Stephen B. Thomas, "The Legacy of Tuskegee," *Body Positive*, February 2000.

Stephen B. Thomas and Sandra Crouse Quinn, "The Tuskegee Syphilis Study, 1932 to 1972: Implications for HIV Education and AIDS Risk Education Programs in the Black Community," *American Journal of Public Health*, November 1991.

Internet Sources

Borgna Brunner, "The Tuskegee Syphilis Experiment," 2003. www.tuskegee.edu/ Global/story.asp?s=1207586.

Stephen Chau and Thomas Liu, "Prejudice in Health Care." www.stanford. edu/class/e297c/poverty_prejudice/sla very_colonialism_reparations/chauliu.

Bill Clinton, "Apology for Study Done in Tuskegee," May 16, 1997. www.clin ton4.nara.gov/textonly/New/Remarks/ Fri/19970516-898.html.

A.W. Fourtner, C.R. Fourtner, and C.F. Herreid, "'Bad Blood': A Case Study of the Tuskegee Syphilis Project." http://ub lib.buffalo.edu/libraries/projects/cases/ blood.

Vanessa Northington Gamble, "Tuskegee Lessons: Syphilis Study Leaves Behind Legacy of Mistrust," National Public Radio, July 25, 2002. www.npr.org/ programs/morning/features/2002/jul/ tuskegee/commentary.

Indiana University, "Factual Basis: An Historical Look at the Tuskegee Study," 2001. www.indiana.edu/~poynter/sas/ lb/facts.html.

Michigan State University, "Faces of Tuskegee." www.msu.edu/course/hm/ 546/tuskegee.htm.

National Commission for the Protection of Human Subjects of Biomedical and Behavioral Research, "Belmont Report," April 18, 1979. http://ohsr.od. nih.gov/guidelines/belmont.html.

National Public Radio, "Remembering Tuskegee," July 25, 2002. www.npr.org/ programs/morning/features/2002/jul/ tuskegee.

News Hour with Jim Lehrer, "An Apology 65 Years Late," May 16, 1997. www.pbs.org/ newshour/bb/health/may97/tuskegee_ 5-16.html.

"The Nuremberg Code," 1947, University of Michigan. www.med.umich.edu/irb med/ethics/Nuremberg/NurembergCode. html.

Online Ethics Center for Engineering and Science, "Case Study 3: The Tuskegee Syphilis Study." www.onlineethics.org/ edu/precol/classroom/cs3.html.

Tuskegee Syphilis Study Legacy Committee, "A Request for Redress of the

Wrongs of Tuskegee," January 1996. www.med.virginia.edu/hs-library/historical/apology/report.html.

U.S. National Library of Medicine, National Institutes of Health, Medical Encyclopedia. http://www.nlm.nih.gov/medlineplus/ency/article/001327.htm

World Medical Association, "Declaration of Helsinki," 1964. www.wma.net/e/policy/ b3.htm.

Index

American Heart Association (AHA), 62, 63

antibiotics, 69
see also penicillin

apology, 87–89, 96

arsenic, 17–18, 25

Associated Press (AP), 82

autopsies, 40, 42–45, 53

"bad blood," 24, 33, 46

Bad Blood: The Tuskegee Syphilis Experiment (Jones), 48, 63–64

Belmont Report, 85

Black Educational AIDS Project, 94

Brandt, Allan M., 69

Brown, William J., 78–79, 81

Butler, Broadus Nathaniel, 84

Buxton, Peter, 77–81

Captain America, 95

Centers for Disease Control (CDC), 77, 82

civil rights movement, 79

Clark, Taliaferro
experiments and
designing, 30–32
methodology/permissions for, 32
outcome of, 61
retirement from, 40
on misleading subjects, 38
on need to study syphilis, 29

Clinton, Bill, 87–89, 93, 96

Communicable Disease Center, 80

Congressional Subcommittee on Health, 85, 86

control groups, 44–45

Cornely, Paul B., 58

Cumming, Hugh W., 15, 42

Cutler, John, 79, 89

Davis, Michael M., 15

Declaration of Helsinki, 71, 79

Deibert, Austin V., 64–65

Delta and Pine Land Company, 15, 16

Depression, 28

Dibble, Eugene H., 48

discrimination. *See* Jim Crow laws; racism

distrust, of medical establishment, 94–95

Division of Venereal Diseases (U.S. Public Health Service), 75, 78, 80

Duval, Merlin K., 82

effects, 92–95

English, W.T., 19

experiments
blacks involved in, 56–57, 59
consequences of, 45
deceit of subjects in, 33–35, 43–45
doctors' objections to, 73–75
extensions of, 45
full name of, 10
impact on subjects of, 76–77
initial time frame for, 32
location of, 12, 22
as moral failure, 96
nontherapeutic nature of, 10, 68, 70–71
ongoing examinations of subjects in, 48–50
original intent of, 32
public reactions to news about, 82
as racist, 48, 80
recruiting candidates for, 23–24
research methods of, 64–67
routine procedures of, 47–50

Picture Credits

Cover: © SYGMA/CORBIS
© Arthur Rothstein/CORBIS, 19
© Bettmann/CORBIS, 5, 8, 12, 14, 29, 62, 66, 69, 76, 84, 92, 93
Centers for Disease Control, 33
Centers for Disease Control/Susan Lindsley, 17, 41
© CORBIS, 23
Don Cravens/Time Life Pictures/Getty Images, 87
© Ellis Richard/SYGMA/CORBIS, 88, 91
Courtesy of the National Library of Medicine, 15, 20, 30, 43, 60, 65, 74, 81
Steve Zmina, 12 (map)
© SYGMA/CORBIS, 9, 25, 34, 38, 44, 46, 51, 52, 56, 63, 77, 83

About the Author

Michael V. Uschan has written over forty books, including *The Korean War*, for which he won the 2002 Council of Wisconsin Writers Juvenile Nonfiction Award. Mr. Uschan began his career as a writer and editor with United Press International, a wire service that provides stories to newspapers, radio, and television. Journalism is sometimes called "history in a hurry"; Mr. Uschan considers writing history books a natural extension of skills he developed in his many years as a working journalist. He and his wife, Barbara, reside in the Milwaukee suburb of Franklin, Wisconsin.